# PAYMENT REFUSED

# PAYMENT REFUSED

## WILLIAM M. SHERNOFF

Richardson & Steirman
New York
1989

ISBN: 0-931933-58-7

L.C.C. Number: 85-073299


Typography by Dawn Typographic Services

Payment Refused by William M. Shernoff is published by
Richardson & Steirman, Inc.
5 West 19th Street, New York, New York 10011.

## *Editorial Note*

Because of the enormous amounts of court testimony and records required to prepare this book, contractions and excerpts have been made for editorial purposes and reasons of clarity. But in no way has the sense or meaning of any testimony been intentionally changed.

The Editors

## Acknowledgements

I wish to thank Thelma O'Brien for helping me with the writing of this book, and Marian Haycock Tully and Dan Williams for helping me with editing the manuscript. Much credit is also owed to my family for their patience and understanding in allowing me to pursue a busy career.

I would be remiss if I did not give thanks to my clients who allowed me to pursue their causes, my office staff, and the many trial lawyers throughout the country who have helped me throughout my career.

William Shernoff

# The Insurance Revolt in California

On November 8, 1988, after a dramatic battle, California residents voted for an upheaval in the insurance industry. With the backing of Ralph Nader and the work of consumer activist Harvey Rosenfield, the people of California passed Proposition 103—an initiative to make the insurance industry more accountable to the will of the people. Its major provisions are as follows:

(1) The office of insurance commissioner will be changed from an appointive position to an elective position. Previously, commissioners were appointed from the insurance industry.

(2) Liability insurance carriers will not be able to increase rates without first obtaining approval from the insurance commissioner.

(3) The insurance industry shall be subject to the consumer protection laws of the state.

(4) A non-profit consumer organization with oversight responsibilities over the insurance industry will be created.

(5) The insurance industry anti-trust exemption will be repealed.

(6) There will be an immediate 20 percent rollback of liability insurance rates (with additional cuts for good drivers) on auto policies.

The workings of insurance profitability will soon be unveiled, since the financial books and records of insurance companies will now come under intense public scrutiny. For example, it may soon become common public knowledge that the leading automobile insurance company, State

Farm, made profits in 1987 of 2.6 billion dollars (that's with a *B*, folks) and has built up an astounding surplus of 13.9 billion dollars.

Insurance is a regulated industry. In order to raise rates, each insurance company is generally required to justify its increases to a state insurance commissioner. Insurance companies love to claim losses when making a case for higher rates to the insurance commissioner. But soon it will be understood that an insurance company's prime source of profit is from *investment income*. The difference between premiums coming in and claims paid out (underwriting results) seldom shows a substantial profit. Insurance companies almost always neglect to mention their huge profits from investments and the gigantic reserve accounts and surpluses they have built up. This kind of deception will no longer be tolerated because this giant industry will now be under the glare of the public eye.

The ink hardly had time to dry on Proposition 103 before the insurance industry challenged the constitutionality of the new law. Although the California Supreme Court has accepted the case for review, it will be some time before it is known whether Proposition 103 will be upheld, in total or in part. Meanwhile, other states are now considering passing laws modeled on Proposition 103. Undoubtedly, insurance reform is on the move.

William M. Shernoff, Esquire
Claremont, California
1989

# Table of Contents

# Foreword
## by
## Ralph Nader

Did you ever try to read those obscure paragraphs in your insurance policy? Did you understand them? Did you ever wonder why they weren't written in clear, simple language? The chances are that you accepted the obscurity and difficult language as just the way these matters have always been. You bought your policy based on the good faith of your insurance company.

Suppose the obscure language is put there to confuse you?

And, when you have a legitimate claim, what makes you believe your insurance company will deal with you in good faith?

The average consumer spends 12 cents out of every income dollar on insurance; therefore one would expect some kind of government regulation over this multibillion-dollar industry. Indeed, every state has an insurance department whose mandate is to regulate and supervise the insurance industry. But, in most instances, state regulation is a farce. State agencies have few actuaries or professional staff to check insurance-company abuse even if the agencies were anxious to protect you in the first place.

In only two or three states at any given time are there insurance commissioners with the desire to curb abuse. Many commissioners, selected because of their knowledge of the industry, usually have close ties to the industry. The annual meetings of the National Association of Insurance Commissioners (NAIC) are replete with hotel hospitality suites and evenings of entertainment hosted by insurance groups or companies—the very companies the commissioners are supposed to regulate. And this is where hordes of insurance executives, lobbyists, and public-relations specialists lavish attention on the state commissioners and their staffs.

Concerned about this state of affairs, late in 1983 consumer groups appealed to NAIC to appoint a consumer advisory committee to balance the avalanche of one-sided information pouring out of the insurance companies.

NAIC turned it down.

If the insurance departments of the various states do not wish to concern themselves with the rights of the consumers—what, if anything, is their function? That is the multibillion-dollar question. The answer is self-evident.

During World War II, the United States Supreme Court ruled that insurance was an interstate business and therefore within federal regulatory purview. But the insurance industry is so powerful that it flexed its lobbying muscles and secured legislation through Congress in 1945 (the McCarran-Ferguson Act), taking the federal government out of insurance regulation.

Too many insurance companies are crass, profit-oriented, and specialize in "bad faith" relationships with the consumer. They engage in all-out battles with the policyholder in two areas:

    (a) behind the scenes as lobbyists;

    (b) when policyholders try to collect on a legitimate claim.

For the past thirteen years, members of Congress have tried to enact legislation to compel greater insurance disclosure to consumers. Disclosure would enable consumers to comparison-shop and obtain the best buy—much as in buying a car. But the industry is so powerful that it has bottled up this effort successfully. It even went so far as to get Congress *to curtail the right of the Federal Trade Commission to study the industry.* Fortunately, now the

General Accounting Office (the investigative arm of Congress) is assessing the inadequacies of state regulation.

Not only is it difficult for the consumer to comparison-shop policies of different companies, but the industry has blocked other sources of competition which could reduce the rate of your insurance. In 50 states insurance agents are prohibited from discounting their premiums to get your business. And in 37 states you and your neighbors are prohibited from getting together as a group and buying—at a lower price—a group homeowners insurance policy.

But a major problem with insurance companies is the legitimate claim. Whether it is a fire in your home, a work-related disability or an accident and your claim is covered by your insurance policy, the question is: Will you collect?

Despite what is written in your policy, the judge of whether you'll be paid is the claims adjuster—not the insurance agent or insurance sales department who may have been taking your money five, ten or even twenty years. The claims adjuster has the power to pay, settle, or not pay at all.

So what happens when your honest claim is turned down?

When small claims are rejected by the adjuster, most people give up in disgust. *This is exactly what the insurance companies want you to do.* Think about the millions of honest claims that are never challenged, and you can understand the surge of wealth generated by most major insurance companies. An angry consumer may seek redress from the state insurance commissioner, but, as explained earlier, this is rarely effective.

Or you can take the insurance company to court.

The man who has rattled more nonpaying insurance companies than anyone else in the country is attorney William Shernoff. His specialty is going after insurance companies who demonstrate "bad faith" in dealing with policyholders. He has won many cases for compensatory and punitive damages for clients who have paid their premiums faithfully—only to find that they had to fight their insurance companies to collect on their injuries. In one case, when Shernoff was able to demonstrate that a major insurance company acted in "bad faith" when it turned down a simple claim, the jury awarded the policyholder $8 million in punitive damages.

While many claims are settled for smaller amounts of money, newspaper and TV coverage of blatant cases have alerted consumers of their rights when they buy insurance coverage.

In this book, *Payment Refused*, Shernoff brings to your attention the unfair policies practiced by these insurance companies. In a series of dramatic case histories, you follow Shernoff as he argues each case before a judge and jury—stripping away the obscure paragraphs and confusing language that insurance companies believe give them license to turn down honest claims.

Take the case of Mike Egan, an Irish immigrant in his early fifties who hurt his back when he fell off a roof. Charging that he was malingering, Mutual of Omaha decided it would make no further payments after three months. Or take the case of Joe Ingram who injured his back on the job. He believed he was covered under a credit disability policy with Commercial Bankers Life Insurance Company. The company decided otherwise.

Ray Pistorius was a long-and short-haul trucker who was injured in an accident just 12 days after he increased his disability policy with Prudential Insurance Company. After months of paying on his claim, the nation's largest insurer suddenly decided to discontinue paying him his monthly benefits.

Ultimately these plaintiffs won their cases. But many policyholders have paid premiums only to discover that they have been turned down on their claims. It is no wonder that in some states, notably California, the courts have been mindful of the people with legitimate claims who have been refused payment. This is the reason for the punitive-damage awards: the high cash awards that punish the insurance companies for refusing to honor their policies. It is a message by the courts that disreputable claims practices must be stopped.

Shernoff feels strongly about the matter. He points out, correctly, that a policyholder who defrauds an insurance company ends up in prison, but an insurance-company official who defrauds a consumer is not even subject to prosecution.

In the absence of organized bargaining power by policyholders, taking companies to court and obtaining punitive-damage awards help fill the void. However, more effective action could be taken by legislative bodies if they would only read the depositions of company officials testifying in court; they verify in their own words how they hoodwink the policyholder.

As Shernoff points out, the initiative for any basic change has to come from the policyholders who are victims and from their advocates. In Chapter 7, Shernoff describes the work of the National Insurance Consumer Organization (NICO), which is battling insurance-industry abuse. It is headed by Robert Hunter, an actuary who was the former federal insurance administrator. NICO is leading the way toward public awareness and action and may be contacted at

NICO
121 Payne Street
Alexandria, Virginia 22314

Under law, insurance companies are fiduciaries, which means that they are founded on public trust. They employ actuaries who calculate and anticipate the income versus claims against the company. This results in a reasonable profit for the insurance companies. However, by a change in outlook, insurance companies decided that they are profit centers. This attitude enabled them to deny or cut down on paying legitimate claims or harass policyholders in order to achieve greater profits. This is a betrayal of trust.

Case by case, Shernoff and other attorneys who battle the "bad faith" of the insurance industry are building the legal shield to protect you from mistreatment.

This book is an important milestone in the fight for consumer rights. It was written so that you may know and understand these rights when you buy an insurance policy. Now, in the pages of this absorbing book, read how interesting the struggle for those rights can be.

Ralph Nader<br>
Washington, D.C.

# Preface

It was a hot, sultry May morning in 1984 when I boarded the DC-9 aircraft that would take me across the white-capped California mountains to Sacramento, the capital of California. For the next several days, we would testify on behalf of consumers against an array of insurance-sponsored bills in the state legislature.

After landing, I found the nearest cab and headed quickly for The Lobby, a restaurant near the Capitol Building, where members of the California Trial Lawyers Association were waiting. As I opened the large wooden door, I recognized several insurance lobbyists.

A nervous young man I did not know in a gray suit and gold-rimmed glasses came up to me and said, "I'm from Blue Cross. You seem to be suing us a lot these days," he said apprehensively and then laughed. He offered his hand.

Somewhat startled, I shook his hand and said, "That's right. Now we're up here to kill your anticonsumer bills tomorrow."

Though civil, the terse exchange illustrates the daily struggle between trial lawyers and insurance companies. It happens in the legislature and in the courts. Ironically, while insurance lobbyists dined upstairs and discussed strategy on how to defeat the trial lawyers, we were meeting downstairs to discuss how to stop their anticonsumer measures. Although the legislature has been the site for many such encounters, during the last decade the battle for consumer rights in the insurance industry has been waged in the courts.

This book, *Payment Refused*, portrays some of those struggles. These are cases about a number of American consumers who possessed the courage and tenacity to seek justice against insurance company abuse by taking them to court.

I've practiced insurance law on behalf of the consumer since the early 1970s. When I began trying these cases, there were hardly any trial lawyers around who had even heard of this emerging new facet in law now called "bad faith." Today, trial lawyers across the country are pursuing bad faith insurance cases on behalf of policyholders. Its development has dramatically affected the legal careers of many trial lawyers who support consumers' rights. The law of bad faith insurance is emerging as a consumer movement of its own and it has shaped my career as a trial lawyer dramatically.

I was raised in the small farming community of Crivitz, Wisconsin, 50 miles north of Green Bay. My family came to Wisconsin from Chicago to escape the lingering effects of the Great Depression of the 1930s. Few jobs existed even for my father, an attorney with degrees from the University of Chicago and De Paul University Law School.

My grandparents, Sarah and William Shernoff, were immigrants who fled the persecution of Russia in the 1920s to try to find a new life in America. They settled in Chicago, where they eventually operated a few pawnshops. This allowed my grandfather, a watchmaker, to work at his trade.

When someone gave my grandparents a piece of land in Wisconsin in exchange for a debt, my family decided to move there and build a farm on the property. The year was 1935, two years before my birth. In 1937, due to the lack of medical facilities in the area, my mother went back to Chicago for the occasion of my birth. When she was able to travel, we returned to the farm.

It was a dairy farm with a barn, cows, chickens, and 400 acres of crops, mostly corn. We didn't make good farmers, so after a short while, my father opened a drugstore 10 miles away in the small village of Crivitz. In addition, he opened up a small law office in back of the drugstore. This career move proved successful because Crivitz's 500 citizens and the region's several thousand farming people were without a drugstore, a lawyer, or a doctor. Besides tending to the drugstore, my father drafted wills and handled the legal problems of the community. During income tax season, it was not unusual for my father to give legal advice to 50 farmers daily. If a farmer couldn't afford the small fee, my father would barter his services for a chicken or some vegetables.

After World War II, we left the farm and added living quarters behind the drugstore. When we moved in, we were the only Jewish family in town. I was eight years old when I began attending the town's grade school. Though I always had friends, I grew up somewhat of a loner because I was unusually shy. I worked in the drugstore and was active in school sports.

Even today, my memories of Crivitz and the town's farming people give me a warm feeling. One reason is best exemplified by a tragic incident that took place in the fall of 1951. One bitter cold night, while my family slept, my mother smelled smoke. She roused me and we barely escaped as flames began to engulf the entire building. Unfortunately, it was deer season, and when deer season begins in northern Wisconsin, most men, including Crivitz's volunteer fire department, are not around. By morning, there was nothing left of the drugstore or our home except smoldering lumber and ashes.

But the people of Crivitz came to our aid. Families offered whatever they could spare: articles of clothing, a toaster, even a refrigerator. The town's Catholic priest offered us his house for one year while my dad rebuilt the store. This generous outpouring of community spirit is something I still cherish today.

After graduating from high school in 1955, I decided to pursue the world outside Crivitz, Wisconsin. I applied to the

University of Miami at Coral Gables, Florida. My friends were somewhat surprised that I was going to college because I was not much of a scholar. Also, I don't recall many Crivitz High students who had gone to college. It was taken for granted that young men finished high school and then went to work on the family farm.

After completing college, I was uncertain about my future. With aspirations of becoming a pilot, I applied to the Air Force only to flunk the eye exam. With my father's guidance, I decided to pursue a career in law. Thus, it was in 1960 at the University of Wisconsin Law School in Madison that I finally began my first serious academic training.

Law school brought big changes into my life. During my first year, I had to study long hours while working at the same time, with a legal aid program. It was also the year I married my college sweetheart, JoAnn Ruggero, whom I met in Miami. She gave up her own college career to go to work and help me through law school. During my second year, I worked at the county district attorney's office. In my final year at law school, I was the assistant to the majority floor leader in the Wisconsin Senate.

I graduated from law school in 1962 and promptly joined the army as a first-lieutenant army lawyer. After briefly studying at the Judge Advocate School in Charlottesville, Virginia, I was assigned to Fort Leonard Wood, Missouri, better known as "Little Korea."

The army practice was interesting and kept me busy defending soldiers in general court-martial proceedings. During the day, I would be advising twenty to thirty GIs about all sorts of legal problems. Then, at night, I would be preparing for courts-martial trial experience, defending everyone from a private accused of going AWOL to majors accused of bigamy. It was one trial after another almost nonstop for three years.

The army's most important contribution to my development as a trial lawyer was in public speaking. I always dreaded speaking in front of groups because I was shy most of my life and self-conscious about not being very articulate. But the army in its wisdom, assigned Larry McDonald of Kansas and me to lecture to some 2,000 new recruits each week on military law as extra duty. Military law is generally boring, and our three-hour sessions began at 7:00 A.M., right after the troops had been drilled for hours on the parade ground. Not only did I have to learn how to conquer my fears about public speaking, but McDonald and I had to learn how to keep them awake. Eventually we discovered that jokes, stories, and humorous anecdotes did the trick, and we got to the point where we had the recruits rolling in the aisles.

With my army duties completed in 1965, I was ready for a change in environment: one that would take me far away from "Little Korea." I had two job opportunities. The first job was in Madison, Wisconsin with a civil law firm which would provide a solid position and future security. The second entailed a move to San Francisco and a temporary job with the National Labor Relations Board (NLRB) and the promise of an exciting, uncharted future in California.

I was still undecided when I rolled up to the junction of Route 66 in a 1960 Ford Falcon towing an orange U-Haul with all our worldly goods and $200 in army pay in my pocket. A right turn at the junction led to Madison, and a left turn led to the West Coast. Finally I turned left and headed southwest toward California on Route 66.

I passed the California bar exams and worked one year with the NLRB when I decided to enter private practice. Maybe my army experience had stirred the need for more excitement and challenge in my legal work. I began researching the newspaper want ads for law openings and found what appeared to be an interesting law firm in Claremont, California, a city thirty-five miles east of Los Angeles. It turned out to be a fine choice.

During the first five years, I handled a great variety of

personal injury cases. My boss, Herb Hafif, was a superb trial lawyer and a great teacher. He prodded me continually to concentrate every facet of my life on trial work and make all my daily experiences—from reading the newspaper in the morning to watching a TV special at night—relate to courtroom dynamics.

My first taste of victory in a bad faith insurance case occurred in 1971—just about the time when the legal concept was in its embryonic stages in California. Otis Drake, fifty-nine, worked on a farm and suffered from a severe case of emphysema. For years he had spread manure over acres of farmland in the valley near Chino, California. Finally, his emphysema became so disabling that he had extreme difficulty breathing and could barely walk.

Drake had a disability policy with Pennsylvania Life and was receiving disability income when suddenly the company cut off his benefits. The carrier said that if Drake could walk even a few blocks, he was not house-confined, and therefore ineligible for disability benefits under policy terms. Drake's lawyer made little progress with the insurance carrier. As he worked on the usual hourly rate—a fee the lawyer knew the poor farmer couldn't afford—he referred Drake to me. I studied the case. Growing up in a farming community, I had an empathy for the hard-working farmer, so I was outraged at the attitude of the insurance company. I agreed to represent Drake on a contingency basis, which means that the lawyer works without compensation, but gets a percentage of any financial award if he wins, nothing if he loses.

Otis Drake was one of the most honest and pleasant individuals I had ever met. I was hoping the jury would fall in love with him and his wonderful wife. But—equally important—I knew that Penn Life's decision was absolutely wrong. After a long trial in San Bernardino County Superior Court, the jury awarded Otis all of his disability benefits, plus $325,000 in punitive damages.

After the *Drake* victory, I began to realize that insurance abuse was widespread. Regulatory efforts by state insurance commissioners were minimal. As I reviewed one victim's story after another, I quickly realized that as long as insurance has been part of the American way of life, policyholders have faced insurmountable odds if they chose to challenge their insurance carriers. In protesting a denied claim, few have come out winners. Otis Drake was one of the first. And those who have dared to fight such gothic giants typically have found themselves mired in cumbersome, complex, and costly legal maneuvers. At best, winning resulted in a policyholder's getting what he or she was initially entitled to, less attorney's fees. The insurance company had nothing to lose because the worst that could happen would be having to pay the claim.

Such lopsided battles are as old as insurance itself. Consider the story of William Gybbons—a life insurance policyholder in sixteenth-century England. Gybbons had signed a year-long contract, and then died unexpectedly, shortly before the calendar year ended. However, the insurer asserted, "twelve lunar months of twenty-eight days apiece" had expired, and, therefore, denied Gybbons's wife the benefits. The family took the case to the English courts and eventually won. Yet, over the next 400 years, the insurance industry has developed thousands of ways to deny legitimate claims.

No wonder the average American has little affection for his insurance company. In one 1982 study by the Council of Better Business Bureaus, insurance companies were ranked eleventh among the top fifteen consumer complaint categories—trailing only such industries as franchised auto dealers and general mail-order companies. Of insurance complaints, 61.7 percent were related to such unsatisfactory service as settlement disputes.

Though few state regulators document complaints adequately, the New York Insurance Department registered

52,200 consumer complaints in a single year.

Insurance is supposed to spread the risk. But, from cases I have investigated, insurance carriers are spreading something other than risk. While the industry continues to amass a huge share of the corporate wealth in America, the average legitimate claimant must rely on his insurer's benevolence for the protection promised by his policy.

Many insurance claims are handled routinely without much trouble. Yet the lack of any meaningful regulation has created a growing climate of abuse toward policyholders. Insurance companies insist they sell protection. But, as soon as a policyholder files a claim, an adversarial attitude sets in. The attitude is that a policyholder is automatically wrong and the insurance company automatically right. Then the carrier can use endless technicalities, exclusions and ambiguities to say "Payment refused." The insurance adjuster always seems to enter the revolving door behind you and come out ahead of you.

Many policyholders settle a claim for less than is due them as a way of life. Rather than being rescued by the heroic images used by insurance companies such as Paul Revere, John Hancock, or Thomas Jefferson, the policyholder becomes victimized by accusations. He or she is charged with dishonesty, arson, malingering, and fraud. Understandably, suddenly the policyholder perceives his insurer as an enemy. Indeed, an individual may have lost his health, house and even family members—and now he faces the loss of his self-respect as he defends himself against the charges of his insurance company.

Isn't it ironic that when we hear about insurance cheats, the first image that comes to mind is the guy who falsified a claim in order to reap a bonanza from his insurance company? The industry public-relations mill creates a phantom American policyholder who stages an auto accident, burns down his house, injures himself to avoid work, and, in extreme cases, even kills off relatives to collect death benefits.

Of course, there is consumer fraud. When it occurs, all consumers suffer—in the pocketbook and in the unnecessary distrust created in the system. A carrier should not have to pay false claims. Insurance agents need time to investigate thoroughly and make a sound and fair decision. But to what extent is consumer fraud—as opposed to insurance fraud—occurring? Are both treated with equal weight under the law?

Just as it is hard to quantify insurance fraud, it is also difficult to quantify consumer fraud. Where it is documented—e.g., by the New York Insurance Departments' Fraud Bureau, there are enormous differences. While the 52,200 New Yorkers complained against unfair insurance behavior in 1983, there was fewer than 3,000 complaints filed for consumer fraud.

If a policyholder inflates property or auto damages, sets his car on fire or commits arson, he is breaking the law and should be punished. Indeed, often a district attorney enters the case and the consumer can end up in jail. But how many insurance adjusters do you know who have been indicted for fraud? White-collar insurance executives—caught in well-documented corporate crime against policyholders—do not end up in jail.

Meanwhile, the honest policyholders—who represent the large majority of consumers—are isolated and vulnerable when confronted with problems collecting legitimate benefits. Who is taking up their cause? Thousands of policyholders write letters of complaint to insurance companies which go largely unanswered. A response is usually double talk, with meaningless standard insurance jargon. Occasionally, letters to state insurance departments may inspire a government bureaucrat to settle a dispute. In most cases, these bureaucrats are ineffective representatives of the consumer.

The federal government established state insurance

commissions to detect potential insurance-company insolvencies as well as ensure honest behavior, but insurance regulators admit they are not equipped to carry out the job. "I'm told that we are one of the better insurance commissions, which is scary," said acting New Jersey Insurance Commissioner, Kenneth D. Merin. Like other state insurance commissions, his department, at the time of this writing, was without computers. Meanwhile, the department was using file boxes to regulate 200 New Jersey-based insurance carriers, including the multibillion-dollar Prudential Insurance Company.

Indeed, until about ten years ago, real discipline and punishment for insurance fraud *against* policyholders was a joke. Then the California courts introduced a powerful legal weapon, and the legal concept of insurance bad faith was born.

The law of bad faith is simple. If a policyholder's claim has been unreasonably denied, he can sue for more than the amount of his benefits. He can collect damages for his mental suffering and all economic loss caused by the company's refusal to honor his legitimate claim. If the insurance company's conduct demonstrates a conscious disregard for the rights of a policyholder, then the policyholder can sue and recover punitive damages. The purpose of punitive damages is to punish and make examples out of companies that engage in outrageous behavior. A jury sets the amount of punitive damages based on the amount of money it will take to make an errant company change and start behaving more responsibly. The larger the company, the larger the amount of punitive damages. A $50 claim may now result in a multimillion-dollar judgment.

The true stories in this book are about honorable people who would not accept denial of benefits by the insurance companies. They told their insurance companies to go to hell, dragged them into court, and asked that they be punished: something that government agencies simply have not done.

In my law practice, I hear insurance horror stories every day. I hear of families hounded by collection agencies to pay medical bills that insurance companies should have paid. I hear of disabled people who are forced to go on welfare instead of collecting disability benefits due them under an insurance policy. In one case, a rental company repossessed a policyholder's wheelchair because the insurance carrier failed to make payments. One woman became so distraught because the company would not pay her medical bills that she attempted suicide. Some businesses, large and small, have gone bankrupt when reluctant insurance companies refused to make timely payments.

The punishment handed out by juries against insurance companies has been beneficial for consumers. Jury verdicts are helping to equalize the power between the large insurance company with its unlimited funds and a heavily staffed legal department and the small consumer. Thanks to bad faith lawsuits, the insurance industry no longer wields the freedom to practice what it pleases on whom it pleases. The law's message is clear: today, those who abuse the free marketplace can be brought to justice and punished severely—not by government, but by the victim.

Originally, when I began challenging insurance companies in court, I thought realistically I would be hitting my head against a stone wall. After all, the insurance industry is part of the American way of life, a necessity in today's world. With its huge financial resources, on numerous occasions in this century, the insurance industry has flexed its political muscle and had its way successfully in Washington and in state legislatures.

However, in the past ten years, as this book documents, legal action by consumers against abuse has influenced profoundly the insurance industry. Insurance companies now complain about the high punitive-damage awards.

Industry argues that punitive awards (as distinguished from compensatory awards for actual losses) are huge windfalls for the victim and his attorney. The industry even has the audacity to threaten to raise premiums because of such punishment.

Such reactions are petulant, at best. Punitive damages are a penalty for outrageous conduct, and most states forbid an insurance company to raise premiums because it was caught in fraudulent activities. In addition, competition within the industry will ensure that decent companies—those that do not defraud—have a cost advantage against those who are forced to pay huge sums for illegal activities.

When the industry is feeling particularly defensive, usually after the widespread media attention of a multimillion-dollar judgment, it counters with a blizzard of press stories against the evils of lawyers. "The contingency fee," they argue, "is ruining the American way of life."

The truth is that the contingency fee is the poor man's way—often the only way—of obtaining justice. When a contingency fee arrangement is made, the client pays the lawyer nothing to handle the case. The lawyer invests his own time, money, and effort and receives payment "when and if" he wins the case which may drag on for years; the fee is usually 30 to 40 percent of the total award. Contingency fee arrangements make it possible for the consumer—of any income bracket—to fight his insurance carrier. At the same time, the method provides an incentive for lawyers to represent good so-called "small-potatoes" cases. All of my cases are based on a contingency fee.

The insurance industry still charges that the large awards are substantial windfalls. In one sense, they are. But they are not nearly the windfalls the industry reaps when it invests policyholders' money after delaying benefit payments. Furthermore, whatever windfalls these awards represent, they also have an undeniable therapeutic effect of making the industry more honest.

Let's face it. It requires a lot of money to fight an insurance company and it requires a carefully trained staff of legal and insurance experts to uncover and pursue insurance fraud. I have used most of the money I've made into building a bigger legal operation. I began alone, and now there are nine lawyers in the firm, four insurance analysts, and a large support staff of paralegals, law clerks, legal secretaries, computer operators, and other professional personnel. The funding for this highly specialized operation originates from the penalties insurance companies pay when they get caught abusing consumers—and I intend to keep on catching them. I believe most citizens prefer this aggressive legal system as long as government regulation is ineffective.

Ironically, it is the insurance industry that has prevented us from reducing the windfall aspects of large punitive awards. I and others have lobbied in the California legislature for laws that would assign a substantial portion of punitive awards to public-interest projects. But the insurance industry—with one of the most effective lobbying operations in the country—has kept such laws off the books. They know that if some of this money is used for public interest projects, that the "windfall" argument would no longer be valid, and that these awards would become more popular with judges, juries, and the public.

Meanwhile, the punitive awards for bad behavior the insurance companies are obliged to pay will ensure that ordinary people are treated fairly by their insurance companies: a policy that aims to preserve basic economic and social rights within a democracy.

# Chapter 1

# The First Big Verdict

On May 11, 1970, Michael Egan, a muscular fifty-five-year old roofer, fell off a ladder. He had begun his day like hundreds before, constructing rooftops in Pomona, California. But this morning, as he stepped down the ladder, a rung broke. Mike plunged 12 feet to the ground, injuring his back severely. Mike's life would never be the same. In the end, the roofer's accident would shake the insurance industry to its very core.

Mike had carried a Mutual of Omaha disability insurance policy for years. The policy promised to pay $200 a month for life if Mike became totally disabled by an accident. Following Mike's mishap, Mutual of Omaha paid benefits, but cut them off abruptly in 1971. By 1973, Mike had no other choice but to sue.

I was thirty-five years old and a partner with the firm of Hafif & Shernoff when I first heard about Michael Egan. I had recently won the Otis Drake case and I was psychologically prepared. I had a gut feeling the Egan case could become a legal rocket.

At about the same time Mike's case was to come to trial, Hafif decided to enter the 1974 Democratic primary for governor of California. His commitment to state politics meant that I had to try most of our cases. I was ready.

The trial reflected a classic confrontation. Mike, a stout Irish immigrant with a grade-school education, worked most of his life as a roofer. He had a disabled wife and a young daughter.

At the other side of the courtroom sat attorneys for Mutual of Omaha, a company self-acclaimed as the largest accident and health insurance company in the world.

In the early days of handling bad faith cases, the insurance companies did not appreciate the dynamics or potential risks of a jury trial. Sometimes I was opposed by lawyers competent in boardrooms and backrooms, but unaccustomed to the "trenches" of the courtroom.

The trial began without fanfare. The nine-story Pomona Courthouse is the biggest building in Pomona, but few people are interested in everyday civil disputes. Civil courtrooms are virtually empty.

Mike's case was simple. He hurt his back falling off a roof. After about six months of conservative therapy, the injury required back surgery. Unfortunately, the operation was unsuccessful, and the doctors declared Mike totally disabled.

Classification of Mike's injury as a *sickness* or an *accident* became the pivotal point in the case because accident payments were for life, and sickness payments stopped in three months. Mutual of Omaha opened Mike's file as an accident claim, but, for mysterious reasons, had converted the accident claim to a sickness claim. The decision to reclassify the claim occurred at about the same time that Mike's total disability became obvious. Having received benefits under the accident classification, the switch meant that Mike would only be eligible for three months of benefits. Mike had no choice but to head straight for the courtroom. The trial was truly a trip into the wild kingdom.

I opened the trial with Michael Egan, his wife Mary, and daughter, Maureen, telling their stories in simple terms. They all made believable and sympathetic witnesses. They told how Mutual's Los Angeles claims manager, Andrew McEachen, came to the Egan home. McEachen said that Mutual had decided to cut Mike's payments off. In his accusations, McEachen charged Mike could work if he wanted to; he was merely malingering.

Upset, Mike denied the manager's accusations. He told the manager that his disability left him distraught about money. With Christmas near, Mike could not even buy his family presents. The family testified that McEachen laughed at Mike during the visit and called him a fraud. Mike, normally a strong man, began to cry. His wife and daughter were there and heard the whole episode. They, too, were distraught. Mike was angry and humiliated.

There was a second personal visit to Mike's home, this time from Mutual claims adjuster Michael Segal. The adjuster argued that Mike's disability had been caused by sickness, and therefore Mike was no longer eligible for disability. Segal then told Mike that if he would surrender his policy, Mutual would give Mike a generous payment. Despite his desperate need for the money, Mike refused.

After Segal's visit, Mike confirmed his diagnosis with Dr. Donald Carpenter, who again classified Mike as totally disabled by his accident. Mike wrote Segal in Los Angeles and requested continued payment of his disability benefits. Mike kept a copy, but never received a response to the letter.

Because his injury had been on the job, Mike had also filed a worker's compensation claim. They gave him a high disability rating. Having exhausted its personal savings, the Egan family lived on worker's compensation.

Mike never returned to work and continued seeking regular medical care. Doctors referred him to a rehabilitation program; but after exhaustive tests, they told him that rehabilitation efforts were impossible. Under extreme financial stress, the Egans eventually had to borrow money in order to live. Here was a family depending upon the good faith of Mutual of Omaha—"the people that pay." Instead it was left in financial shambles and emotional chaos when Mike tried to collect his claim.

I next called Mike's attending doctor, Dr. Stephen Odgers,

to the stand. Dr. Odgers explained Mike's severe medical condition, his surgery, and explained how Mike's condition was attributed to his fall.

Next, the jury needed to hear from Mutual of Omaha. Surely they had some excuse for treating Mike this way. I first called Segal as an adverse witness. I wanted to dispense with two points quickly to set the foundation for the questions to follow. First, I wanted to make it clear that Mike was totally disabled. Donald Wild and Alfred Doutre, the two lawyers who tried the case for Mutual, sat at counsel table and looked concerned as I started my cross-examination

Shernoff: "There was no question that Mr. Egan was totally disabled as far as the policy goes?"

Segal: "Right. I don't believe the question of total disability ever was raised."

Q. "It was just accident versus sickness?"

A. "Yes."

Next, I had to quickly destroy Mutual of Omaha's possible argument that some sort of sickness, such as arthritis, was involved in Mike's disability. I proceeded directly with pointed, leading questions.

Shernoff: "Osteoarthritis means degenerative wear and tear, doesn't it?"

Segal: "Yes."

Q. "And you would not classify the normal wear and tear of a person's spine such as we all have as we grow old, the aging process or, as Dr. Odgers indicated, gray hair or wrinkles in the skin—you wouldn't classify that as a sickness or a disease such as to deprive someone of their benefits, would you?"

A. "No, of course not, sir."

Throughout the trial, Segal had argued that the home office had decided to deny Mike's claim. I was sure that Segal would try to blame someone in the home office. At this point in the trial, I intended to prove that fact through his testimony.

Shernoff: "Sir, could you tell me how this incident of falling off of a ladder onto your back necessitating surgery some nine months later and which your company originally opened up as an accident claim could somehow, in your mind, become a sickness?"

Segal: "Well, it wasn't in my mind. And this was based on medical and file information that the company had had, and it was reviewed, and this is the suggested handling."

Q. "Isn't it true, sir, that someone in the company directed you to handle the claim in that particular fashion, and that is what you did?"

A. "I was directed in all cases."

Q. "I am talking about this case at this time. We will get to some other cases later on."

A. "Well, that would include this case, too."

Q. "Isn't it a fact, sir, that someone in a supervisory position directed you to handle the file in this manner?"

A. "Yes."

Q. "Who was that?"

A. "I would not know at this time."

Q. "Why not?"

A. "Because, unfortunately, it did not indicate the name of the person who instructed me thus."

In a report back to the home office, Segal had concluded with the phrase "best to handle on the basis of sickness." I seized upon that statement. I intended to demonstrate that the classification conversion from "accident" to "sickness" devastated Mike and profited Mutual of Omaha by a tidy sum.

Shernoff: "Now, you have this phrase here, down three lines from the bottom, 'Best to handle on the basis of sickness.'"

Segal: "Yes."

The jury looked at Segal; they could anticipate my next question. At this point, Segal was rather sober.

Q. "Now, at that time you wrote that you, of course, knew that if you handled it on the basis of sickness you would be depriving Mr. Egan of some twenty years of benefits and that he would only receive three months' benefits; is that correct?"

A. "Well, I base claims on—on facts, not— when I base—but, I mean, I handle claims on the information."

Q. "Excuse me.... the question was, at the time you wrote that—"

A. "Yes."

Q. "—you knew you had knowledge of the fact that if you handled it on a sickness he would be cut off after three months?"

A. "Yes."

Q. "Okay. Now, when you said 'Best to handle on basis of sickness,' what did you mean by that? Was this best for Mr. Egan?"

A. "No."

Q. "Now, this decision to close on the basis of sickness is really quite an important decision from the company's standpoint, is it not?"

A. "Yes."

Q. "As a matter of fact, we can figure it out mathematically. It amounts to about a $40,000 decision, doesn't it?"

A. "As I look at it now, yes, sir." [He admitted with a pause.]

Q. "And the $40,000 decision, certainly with your experience with the company, is quite carefully reviewed by people in high authority, is it not?"

A. "Well, I would say generally most files are reviewed."

Having pried these admissions out of Segal, I proceeded to pound away on how little investigation Segal had carried out to determine whether Mike's disability originated from a sickness or an accident. I wanted to show that Mutual of Omaha did not want a thorough investigation; with hardly any evidence, the carrier could rush through a reclassification with the sole purpose of saving money. Segal went a long way toward proving my point.

Shernoff: "Well...just let me ask you this. In all

fairness, you are cutting this man's benefits off on the basis of some sickness in his back just shortly after you know he has surgery. Did you at least check, let's say, with his doctor who had been treating him for eight or nine years to see whether or not his doctor would agree that some disease process was going on?"

Segal: "No, that wasn't done."

Q. "Did you check with the doctor who did the surgery on his back or ask the doctor who performed the surgery whether in his opinion the surgery was necessitated by the fall or whether the surgery was due to some sort of rare disease?"

A. "Well, I didn't check myself, no, sir."

Q. "Wouldn't that have been the proper thing to do, sir?"

A. "I believe so."

Q. "Having looked at the file and having sat here the best part of the day and answered questions, do you have any opinion as to whether or not this claim was handled properly on the 19th of May, 1971?"

A. "Well, I have pondered this considerably, and I feel there could have been some more handling done at that time."

Q. "If you had it to handle at the present time, and if you have any opinion, how would you handle it?"

A. "Well, for sure I would make certain that

the doctors were contacted and, perhaps, an independent medical examination would be suggested and done. Perhaps. And further review by a medical department, by our medical department, claims department."

Segal's testimony placed Mutual of Omaha in a real bind. The jury had already seen the Egan family and how they had suffered considerably at the company's hands. Surely, the jury thought, Mutual of Omaha must have some kind of plausible excuse. But here was Segal, virtually admitting that Mike's reclassified claim from accident to sickness had little justification—except to save the company $40,000. Segal admitted that there was little investigation, but would not take the blame himself; he insisted that others directed him to do it. Well, if he wasn't responsible, who was? The jury wanted to know.

I next called Segal's boss, McEachen—who didn't help Mutual of Omaha either. He said he did not harass Mike in his home, but the jury did not believe him. When I shot a direct question at him about whether the termination of Egan's benefits was right or wrong, McEachen became flustered; he stuttered and stammered.

Shernoff: "You know Mr. Egan's benefits were terminated, what might have been lifetime benefits, were terminated on the basis of sickness, do you not?"

McEachen: "Yes, I do."

Q. "Do you feel that the action by the company was wrong?"

A. "I feel that you have this—"

He paused a long time. I started to get restless. He said, "I think that—" and paused again.

Q. "Can he answer yes or no, Your Honor?"

The Court: "I think you can answer the question, please, Mr. McEachen."

The judge was waiting, too. And finally from the witness:

A. "There could be a question, yes. I meant, could be more information that may be necessary in order to—but this is hindsight, I mean. Truly I mean, maybe I am kind of dense."

I felt a sense of relief after this testimony. McEachen obviously attempted to perform his best to justify Mutual of Omaha's conduct, but the truth became so obvious that he simply fell apart. He concluded by saying, "Maybe I am kind of dense." Everyone knew what he really meant. His conduct simply couldn't be justified for any other reason. But McEachen was not dumb. He tried to play the role, but he was quite unconvincing.

Another claims analyst, Frank Romano, was also persuaded to admit that Mutual's investigation was pathetic, at best.

Shernoff: "Can you tell us why Dr. Carpenter wasn't consulted about this?"

Romano: "No, sir, I can't tell you why he wasn't consulted."

Q. "Can you tell us why Dr. Odgers wasn't consulted?"

"No, sir, I can't."

Q. "Can you tell us why action was taken to terminate Mr. Egan's benefits without consulting one medical doctor?"

A. "No, sir, I can't."

Q.  "That's quite improper, isn't it?"

A.  "It would be wrong, I believe, yes."

Now, I had completed the circle. All three adjusters admitted that the insurance carrier's actions were wrong. Mutual of Omaha's attorneys realized the obvious: their strategy now was to turn against the local adjusters, Segal and McEachen, and try to cut them loose. The home office knew nothing of this travesty, argued the attorneys. If the strategy worked, the jury might sympathize with an honest company that simply had two rotten eggs.

The trial's focus shifted. The question became: who was responsible for the dirty work—the local adjusters or the home office? Everyone at Mutual of Omaha pointed the finger at someone else. I was content to let the testimony stand. Segal maintained he had been directed by someone in a supervisory position. I knew that Mutual of Omaha had to bring in someone from the home office.

Mutual of Omaha did just that by calling in Willard Gustin, the home office manager of the continuing Disability Benefits Department. Gustin took the stand and explained that the authority to terminate claims like Egan's rested with local adjusters. The home office file on Egan, he added, had been misplaced mysteriously. It was just lost somewhere, "as can happen in large corporations," for a period of time. The file must have fallen in a "corporate crack," for a while, he said. This "corporate crack" threatened to swallow Mutual when I confronted Gustin in cross-examination and made his story fall apart piece by piece.

First, I showed that Mike had written a letter to the home office complaining about the reclassification. That letter was not in the home office file, and its absence was suspicious. Then I tried to show that even if the file had fallen in a crack—back at the home office—they certainly should have discovered it in response to an inquiry from the

Department of Insurance some nine months before the lawsuit was filed. This line of questioning took Gustin somewhat by surprise, and he could not give a very good explanation.

> Shernoff: "Sir, even if it fell into that crack, if someone would specifically call your attention to it, then there would be an analysis. Right?"

> Gustin: "Absolutely."

> Q. "So, sir, isn't it true that in this case Mutual of Omaha's attention was called to this very situation at least one year before this lawsuit was filed by the Department of Insurance, State of California, and to this day your company hasn't responded to that request?"

He didn't reply.

> Q. "Is that true, sir?"

> A. "The only thing I know about this file is what is here."

> Q. "Let me show you a letter addressed to Mutual of Omaha to the attention of Mr. R. C. Olds, Manager, Benefits Service Appraisal Department, July 7, 1972, State of California, Department of Insurance, Ronald Reagan, Governor, signed by Richards D. Barger, Insurance Commissioner, reference Michael Egan."

I showed him the letter. He took it in both hands.

> A. "All right."

> Q. "Sir, isn't it true...that approximately nine months before this lawsuit was

filed, the Department of Insurance called
the attention of Mutual of Omaha to a
complaint filed in this case with reference to Mr. Egan? Didn't they ask you to
actually look into it, analyze it, and
report back to them within 15 days?"

A. "Yes, sir."

Q. "Okay. Let me just ask you this question,
sir. Do you know whether a report was
sent back, if an analysis was done and
sent back to the Department of Insurance as requested either within 15 days
or to this very day?"

A. "I don't know anything about it."

Q. "Certainly should have been done,
should it not, sir?"

A. "I would—" [He stammered again and
paused]. "I can only answer this way,
that upon the receipt of this letter it
should have gone to one of the staff in
the department that handles this sort of
thing."

Q. "Certainly as of that date, even if the file
fell in that deep wide crack, someone
would be obliged to pick it up and
analyze it and see what happened; is that
right?"

A. "It would appear so."

The corporate crack theory began to shrink. How could
Mike's file be misplaced at the home office? First Mike had
written a letter complaining, and then the state
Department of Insurance had made an inquiry. All this
happened before the lawsuit and, surely, someone must

have looked at the file to see what was going on. Furthermore, I knew that I had written a letter offering to settle the case without a lawsuit if the company would restore Mike's disability benefits and pay attorneys' fees. Surely these events would have alerted home office personnel. Yet Gustin stuck to his story tenaciously: the local level did the dirty work, home office really didn't know what was going on.

This line of defense came to an immediate halt with a quirk of fate. When Mutual's lawyer questioned Gustin, he referred innocently to a "file jacket." I had the entire claims file in my possession and I had never heard of, nor had ever seen a file jacket! When it came time to recross Gustin, I pounced upon this file jacket testimony.

Shernoff: "Now, sir, with reference to that particular file, I notice on your direct testimony that you alluded to the fact that there was a jacket usually on those claims file; is that correct.

Gustin: "A green jacket that is a facing type of thing, yes."

Q. "So, in the normal course of business, if we had the notations on the jacket, we would know who saw the file at what times?"

A. "Well, yes and no...It may be a very clean jacket, in which you could go right down the line and find out, boom, boom, boom, boom, who had it when and where. I think the only point that I am trying to make is this: I don't think you can dogmatically make a statement, you know, that this is a hundred percent."

Q. "In your opinion, sir, would it be an

important part of the file itself, this jacket, to be able to determine, within the variances that you have testified to, who saw it and when?

A. "Possibly. I am not sure. I am not sure, really, whether it would or not. Really, the proof of the pudding is in the file."

Q. "Well, the proof of the pudding is in the file but...there seems to be some questions as to who saw it on what dates and even though it is like you say, it may be subject to human error?"

A. "Yes, but the—the thing of it is...now we have got initials that you can recognize by the very nature of the way the man makes the initials; whereas, with a line drawn through a name, you can't really place an identity on a line."

We were not getting very far with this questioning. I wanted the file jacket.

Q. "Do you know where the jacket of that file is?"

A. "Well, it should be—I don't know where it is, if this is what you are asking me, no."

Shernoff: "This was represented to us as a full and complete file."

I showed the court my copy, but it did not have the critical file jacket. I turned to the witness.

Q. "As far as the file back at Mutual of Omaha, it is usually kept in the jacket, is it not?"

A. "Yes, and—"

Q. "And is there ever any reason to take the file out of the jacket?"

A. "Well, if—"

Q. "Except maybe to come to court?"

I knew there was something here, and I could not wait to see this file jacket.

The jury knew there was a file jacket that might expose who saw the file in the home office, when, and perhaps for what purpose. Mysteriously absent from Mutual's original documents, the file jacket was in Omaha. The court ordered the company to produce it immediately, and it arrived by air courier the next day.

I got to court a few minutes early that day, so I asked the court clerk if a package had come in. The clerk found it and I headed upstairs to the cafeteria for a cup of coffee.

When I first read the file jacket, I could hardly believe my eyes. I had hit pay dirt. During the entire trial, Mutual of Omaha had harped on its assertion that its home office had not seen this file during the crucial period around May 1971. However, within that period, the company had reclassified Mike's claim from accident to sickness. And, during those six months, Mike, the Department of Insurance, and I had all protested.

Now, we had a file jacket with approximately twenty dated stamps during that crucial period. In other words, at least twenty times during those critical six months, various people had looked at the file and signed it with their initials. Most amazingly, in May 1971, when the company terminated Mike's claim, it appeared that the file had actually been audited in the home office.

Ten minutes later my coffee was cold, and it was time to return to the courtroom. I grabbed the file jacket and raced down the marble hallways of the courthouse. I found the elevator excruciatingly slow. When the trial finally got underway, I cautiously approached Gustin. I held up the file jacket and as the jurors looked on I asked:

Shernoff: "We can safely say, then, even before this lawsuit was filed in February of 1973, that the people back at Mutual of Omaha looked at their file or wanted to look at their file and actually did look at their file, according to the jacket, probably at least twenty times; is that correct?"

Gustin: "For one reason or another."

Then I zeroed in on the file jacket. Gustin had no choice but to admit what the file jacket said plainly.

Q. "I see here under the box of 'Audit' a checkmark, 6/23/71 with someone's initials. What does the term 'Audit' mean?"

A. "Well, this has to do with the function of the people in the Claims Audit Section, and these labels are—are initialed by those people in that area."

Q. "Which area is that?"

A. "In this Claims Audit Section here."

It now appeared Mutual of Omaha had sunk into its own corporate crack. The jury must have believed that the company didn't treat Michael Egan very fairly in the first place. Now Mutual's attempt to shove all the blame on its lower-echelon adjusters was exposed. The jury's anger seeped into the small dark courtroom as Mutual of Omaha's strategy unraveled slowly.

Incredibly, Gustin grasped at one last straw. He tried hopelessly to explain away the significance of the word "audit."

Shernoff: "In general, in fairness, the word 'audit' would be to see whether things were properly handled, would it not?"

Gustin: "Well, as long as it's understood that I am not talking about any analyzation of what was done. This is strictly a clerical function."

Q. "In other words, when your company uses the word 'audit,' you use it in a much different sense than we ordinarily think of audit like an IRS audit or some other audit? It means something different to the people of Mutual of Omaha than it does to the rest of the world?"

A. "It certainly is used differently, yes."

As Gustin said this, he looked at the jury. They stared at him in disbelief.

Q. "In any event, it appears that somebody did audit the file on 6/23/71; is that correct?"

A. "Yes, sir."

I knew then the case was going beautifully. Did he really think that the jury would believe that Mutual of Omaha used the word "audit" differently than the rest of the world!

My last task was to produce evidence of Mutual of Omaha's financial worth and to sum up. In a punitive damage case, a jury can hear evidence of the company's worth in order to set the appropriate punishment.

Every state insurance department requires insurance companies conducting business in that state to file a complete yearly financial report. It is public record and shows detailed financial information about every insurance company; including all assets, liabilities, net worth, and income for the preceding year. In order to show the jury Mutual of Omaha's financial condition, I had subpoenaed those annual reports. I wanted the jury to receive a complete and up-to-date financial picture of Mutual of Omaha's assets.

Mutual's lawyers were not content to let these statements speak for themselves. In 1973 and 1974, economic times were not the best for insurance companies, and it was true that Mutual of Omaha's income was down a bit, as was most insurance income in those fluctuating years. The company introduced Mutual of Omaha's comptroller, Marvin Maher, in a futile attempt to convince the jury that Mutual of Omaha faced hard times. After all, Mutual of Omaha wasn't that big, they argued.

But Maher overplayed his hand. His testimony opened the door for me to reveal another of Mutual's attempts to pull the wool over the juror's eyes. I began cross-examination with the last annual report on file with the California Department of Insurance.

Shernoff: "Okay. Now, sir, let's get to the assets of this company as we are talking about the California statement now. Give us the total assets of this small company, sir."

Maher: "The total assets are $756,596,000. I have rounded that off. Do you want it complete?"

Shernoff: "Yes, sir."

Maher: "All right. Let's start again. $756,596,693.17."

Q. "As I understand it, of that $756,000,000, you have got how much in bonds that you have invested in?"

A. "$556,335,745.24."

Q. "And how much in preferred stocks?"

A. "In preferred stocks, $23,982,503.23."

Q. "And how much in common stock?"

A. "In common stock, $152,180,159.48."

Q. "How about just plain old cash on hand?"

A. "Cash, $15,953,954.58."

Q. "Now, sir, can you tell us the net gain from operations before dividends to policyholders and before federal income taxes and excluding capital gains and losses for the year, the operational year 1973?"

A. "It was $27,153,394.92."

Q. "So, as I understand that figure, that twenty-seven million dollars, that is what the net profit or net gain was of the company in 1973 before you take off dividends to policyholders and income taxes; is that correct?"

A. "That is right, sir."

Q. "You did pay a dividend to life policyholders that has to be subtracted from that. Is that correct?"

A. "Yes, that was $254,653.98."

Q. "And dividends on accident and health policies. How much did you pay on that?"

A. "We paid zero on that."

Q. "Right. Perhaps you can answer this question for me. And before we get to the taxes, it appears that you made some $27,000,000 in 1973. Could you explain to us why no dividends were paid to people who owned the accident and health policies?"

A. "Well, it is just our policy not to pay a cash dividend to them."

Q. "So, your net gain is how much?"

A. $26,898,740.94."

Q. "And of this—out of this $26,000,000 profit in 1973—$26,898,000, how much did you pay in federal income taxes that year?"

A. ''The amount incurred was $2,391,776.91."

Q. "That would be about ten percent, sir?"

A. "That would be approximately, yes."

Q. "So, after the income taxes and after the dividends and after everything in the year 1973, you still had how much left over in profit?"

A. "$24,506,964.03."

The jury got the picture. Mutual of Omaha was not a small and vulnerable company. Rather, the finances reflected exactly what Mutual of Omaha advertised—the company was one of the largest accident and health insurance companies in the world. The figures showed $24 million net profit at the end of 1973, after dividends and taxes.

Dividends and taxes were significant figures, too. Taxes were 10 percent. Most people on the jury paid substantially more than 10 percent in federal income taxes, and I knew they would wonder why a company that made $26 million per year paid only approximately 10 percent in taxes. It was also startling that Mutual of Omaha paid no cash dividends to its accident and health policyholders. After all, a mutual company is owned by the policyholders—at least in theory—and they should be getting a yearly dividend out of the profits. Although the life policyholders received a cash dividend, the accident and health policyholders—representing 90 percent of the business—did not. I delved into these points with Maher. I wanted to show the jury where all the money was really going and how much Mutual of Omaha had amassed in its surplus account.

The surplus account in insurance company accounting is the rough equivalent to the net worth of the company. All of this financial material can get boring, so I had Maher fill in figures on a diagram. I referred to the annual report again and asked Maher:

> Shernoff: "Well, perhaps I can do it by question and answer and everybody could follow it easier. The first figure is surplus funds?"
>
> Maher: "That is correct."
>
> Q. "And what is that figure? Approximately a hundred and forty-four million; is that correct?"
>
> A. "That is correct."
>
> Q. "The next entry is unassigned surplus of December 31st, the previous year." [Maher went over to a diagram and wrote $49,896,240.]

The effect of this testimony was dramatic. We had already proved Mutual of Omaha's net profit for 1973 was $26 million, and now the jury heard Mutual had amassed $145 million in its surplus account at the end of 1973. The testimony revealed that Mutual of Omaha even designated $49 million of it as "unassigned surplus." I made hay out of that in my closing argument. With tongue in cheek, I told the jury that if Mutual of Omaha had so much surplus— some of which they designated "unassigned"—perhaps the jury could assign a portion to the Egans by way of punitive damages.

Maher reviewed two or three additional financial statements, and even though there were fluctuations year to year, Mutual of Omaha's gigantic size permeated Maher's testimony like an expanding balloon. I persuaded Maher to admit that whenever the Dow Jones stock index goes up a few points, Mutual makes a few million. Perhaps the most devastating part of Maher's cross-examination surfaced as I concentrated on Mutual of Omaha's failure to pay cash dividends to the accident and health policy holders. The financial statement for 1973 showed the surplus account up to about $200 million. After having Maher explain all these figures using the blackboard, I had him return to the witness stand.

Shernoff: "Now, sir, I have a few questions that I would like to ask that would not necessitate you standing any longer. You testified yesterday—now, this surplus account, you don't, as I understand it, give any of this surplus, this $200,000,000 or whatever the figure, $100,000,000, $150,000,000, I don't care, you don't give that back to these accident and health policyholders by way of distribution or dividends, do you?"

Maher: "Yes, sir, we do."

Q. "You indicated yesterday you only give them a rider."

A. "I indicated yesterday we do not return money to them in the form of a dividend per se as a person knows or is familiar with. That, you pay out of dividend in cash. We do offer a travel accident death rider as a part of the additional coverage on their policy, and this is, as I said yesterday, given to the policy owners at no increase in their premium."

Q. "You can't spend that, can you sir?"

A. "Yes, sir."

Q. "Can you go in a grocery store and buy groceries with that?"

A. "Yes, sir, the beneficiary can."

Q. "If he has an accident."

A. "If the beneficiary's spouse has an accident."

Q. "Right, but if you don't have an accidental death, you can't spend it?"

A. "Right. That is true."

Q. "And, as a matter of fact, as far as dividends or distributions to the policyholders in what we consider the normal sense of someone getting a dividend, getting money back, getting a check and, as you have so stated on your reports, there is no distribution or dividend of this surplus money, cash to the policyholders?"

A. "That is correct."

Q. "And the policyholders as you have indicated own about 90 percent of the company? In other words, they represent 90 some percent of the income?"

A. "The policy owners own our entire company. And every cent that we show as surplus belongs to our policy owners."

Q. "They don't get a nickel of it, of the cash? And I would like to ask you, sir, who makes the money that this company profits by? In other words, who's getting the money? Do you know, sir?"

A. "The money is staying right into the company for the protection of the policyholders, yes, sir."

Q. "Sir, isn't it a fact that your chief executive officer last year was paid $409,499.02?"

A. "I have no idea what the remuneration or salary compensation was of our—"

Q. "You have no idea?"

A. "No, sir, I don't."

Q. "Doesn't that go in the annual report?"

A. "It does sir, but I do not see that."

Q. "That's a surprise to you?"

A. "It is of little concern to me what our chief executive's salary is."

Q. "Sir, let me show you the complete annual statement that is filed with the Department of Insurance, State of California, which has been marked Plaintiff's Exhibit No. 21 for identification and refer you to the exhibit on the salaries of the officers and it is schedule G and call your attention to, sir, the salary of a Mr. V. J. Skutt. He is the chairman of the board, right?"

A. "That is correct, sir."

Q. "And he got $124,000 plus $284,500?"

A. "That is correct, according to that report, sir."

Q. "And, sir, isn't it true that there are four corporate officers, the secretary and the treasurer, vice-president, and that they received $200,000."

A. "Sir, I repeat, I am not aware of what any of the company officers make. This is not common knowledge to me. If it is in—if they're listed there, then that is an official document, right, that is given to the Insurance Department. This information is not available to me."

Q. "The very first page, that, sir, lists and indicates how many vice-presidents this company has, does it not?"

A. "Yes, sir."

Q. "There are 53 of them, aren't there?"

A. "Well, I didn't count them, sir. I can if you would like for me to."

Q. "I don't think we can take the time, the jury can count them. That is in evidence. That represents over $2,000,000 in salaries, does it not?"

A. "Sir, I do not know. I do not know what the salaries are of these officers."

Q. "Well, we know, sir, that the money isn't going to Mr. Segal, a District Claims Manager, who's making $1,032 a month. He has been with the company ten years. He sure isn't getting much of that money, is he?"

Mutual of Omaha's lawyer stood up. "Objection, Your Honor. Again, I don't—He is just arguing with the witness and making speeches." Well, maybe I was, but the point was made.

Q. "Now, sir, the policyholders of this company, the so-called owners as we have already indicated get no cash distribution, all they really get, sir—all they really have is a hope and a promise if they get injured or sick that the company will pay them in accordance with the policy; is that right?"

A. "Well, sir, I would like not to refer to them as the so-called policy owners. In a mutual company we recognize them as the policyholders. To answer your question: yes. This is why they took out the insurance, as protection. Now, I would like to add—"

Q. "Like Mr. Egan did?"

A. "Sir?" [Maher seemed a little surprised.]

Q. "Like Mr. Egan did?" [Again, same question.] He is an owner, isn't he?"

A. "Yes, sir."

My voice was filled with indignation as I finished. The jury heard what had happened to Michael Egan. Now they knew the company made a handsome profit, possessed a surplus account of about $200 million at the end of 1973, and paid no cash dividends to accident and health policyholders. The company's feeble effort to explain the substituted dividend of a small accident travel death policy did not go very far. This type of policy, I quickly pointed out, cost Mutual of Omaha very little actual dollars.

So, where did the money go? It certainly wasn't distributed back to the policyholders. And from what the jury heard, policyholders like Mike did not receive a fair shake on claims either. The government received little from Mutual of Omaha in the form of taxes. Nor did the company's employees receive much of the income. Segal, a ten-year veteran, made only about $15,000. Indeed, it appeared obvious that most of the company's fortune either went to its high executives in salaries and benefits, or was stockpiled in Mutual's surplus account.

Closing arguments are very important because they give the lawyers not only the opportunity to review the factual evidence, but also to suggest ways to punish the company. I knew that the judge's instruction to the jury on punitive damages would tell them to consider not only Mutual of Omaha's financial worth, but the responsibility of the company's conduct. He would also say that punitive damages should bear a reasonable relationship to actual damages.

This jury was composed of upper-middle-class people who had some business orientation themselves: a sophisticated jury with some understanding of the business world. Some jurors were engineers from a nearby General Dynamics plant. There was a woman on the jury who had worked for insurance companies and owned a Mutual of Omaha policy. I wanted her on the jury because I thought it would be good to let a policyholder see how the company treated someone who filed a claim. I recognized I had to appeal to the jurors' sense of logic and their sense of fairness.

"If it please the Court and Counsel, ladies and gentlemen of the jury. I guess we have all rested in the technical sense, but I haven't rested, and I don't think I will rest until you people come back to this courtroom with a verdict. And then I guess I probably won't even rest after that, but I will rest a little bit easier, I hope.

"This is the time when an attorney has the opportunity to argue or sum up the case—they call it the closing argument. I would like to think that I will be talking with you for a little while. I think this is probably the second most important talk I have ever made of this type in my life; the first being about fifteen years ago when I proposed to my wife. It was kind of like this, because I did a lot of talking, she did a lot of listening, and probably took just as long. But this definitely is the second most important talk I have ever made, ever probably will make in the future, and I think when I am through you are going to know that's true.

"You know what this case involves. The case really transcends Michael Egan. He is involved in it, but it is not only for Michael Egan and, as you will see, the case has implications far and wide. You twelve people sitting there are going to decide this case, and a civil case only takes nine to reach a verdict, nine people sitting in that box who to me and to a lot of people are the nine most important people in the world right now. You have heard all the evidence—you haven't seen all the evidence because a lot of it came in by way of documents, which you will be allowed to take into the jury room with you and examine. And after the arguments of both counsel, this Court, the Honorable Judge, will give you the law that pertains to this case. And your job will be to apply the facts to the law and render a just and fair verdict as you see it.

"Now, in this case we have an obvious situation. A man. A hard-working man, who really never took a dime from anybody in his life. All his life really involves, like most people, is working hard for his family, doing what he is trained and experienced to do. He asks nothing of anybody that he doesn't deserve.

"One day he falls off a ladder. It puts him out of commission for the rest of his life, basically, certainly as a roofer and probably just about for any job on the open labor market that he is trained for and is within his experience and background. An obvious accident, obvious to anybody. I mean, you don't have to have medical training to know that [falling off a ladder] is an accident. Certainly, if you have been in the insurance claims business for a long time, you know that is an accident. It is obvious this man was disabled by this accident.

"Here we have a company, a large company, probably—well, those figures we heard about—I don't know what sums you people are used to dealing with, but those figures to me are something that you read about, hear about.

"What do they do to Michael Egan?

"There was no big problem, for awhile, while they thought it was not a very big claim. They delayed a little bit, maybe there was an excuse for some of the delays, maybe someone was on vacation, you know, things like that can happen. From May up through just before he had his surgery, not too much wrong with the file, nothing very significant.

"Then when it becomes obvious that this is a claim that may be a lifetime benefit, that may expose the company to $40,000 worth of benefits, that's the time that all of a sudden a conversion classification is made to sickness.

"They go out to this man's house—I mean, what does a man have left other than his home and dignity? They go to his house and call him a phony and a fraud and harass him right in his home in front of his wife and his child. It leaves them all crying. The company set up a nonexistent dispute so that perhaps, maybe, they can get him to surrender his policy...That's not decent, it's not right, it's reprehensible. It is outrageous. It is deplorable. It makes you sick. It makes me sick.

"I know there are people who are going to say, well, you know, there's a lot of rip-offs around here, people get ripped off every day...That's true. But, you know, when the people who get ripped off are sick, are disabled and can't fight back because of their physical disability, they're financially down, and then the people who are doing it to them are the powerful people who should know better, that is even more reprehensible.

"I guess the company must know that 999 out of a thousand people in that kind of shape couldn't afford an attorney anyhow.

"You can get away with things for a long period of time, but sooner or later you may get caught...and you get exposed. And sooner or later you get dragged kicking, fighting, whatever, in front of twelve people, twelve people who come from diverse backgrounds, who sit and listen and say what's right and wrong."

It was obvious that I was angry and that I perceived Mutual's treatment of Mike to be outrageous, but I wanted to make sure that this business-minded jury would not get the idea that I am antibusiness. I had to put this case in its proper context.

"Let me stop right here, because I think some people may be saying, Bill Shernoff, you really must be antibusiness. Well, that is not true. There are a lot of good businesses around, and there are a lot of good insurance companies around. A lot of them are making money honestly. Every honest, decent insurance company wants the unscrupulous ones to be punished. And I am not even saying there aren't good and decent people in this company. I am sure there are. But the point is there is a cancer there somewhere. You are the surgeons, and I am going to ask you to cure it."

I then reminded the jury of the so-called "corporate crack."

"The impression that has been paraded around here to you good people has been okay, we did something wrong, we may have handled the file improperly, but, you know, like we just didn't know about it back in the home office, or somehow it got lost in that big corporate crack and kind of went down there, you know, and gee, nobody was handling it or nobody knew about it. Like the first time we heard about this was in this courtroom, you know. That is the impression that they were trying to convey in this courtroom. But we know how false that is."

I finished my summary of the factual evidence by mocking Mutual of Omaha's attempt to minimize its financial worth. My comments were direct and sarcastic.

"The last insult is when it comes time to take into consideration the company's wealth and assets to determine what the appropriate punishment would be. They bring in evidence that this is a small company. They want you to believe that they're going broke or they're losing money. Do they really believe that everybody in this world is a fool?"

After commenting on the evidence and asking the jury to compensate Mike Egan by awarding him his disability benefits and a fair amount for mental and emotional distress, I turned to the critical area of punitive damages. I first discussed the law of punitive damages with the jury

"Now, we get to the second kind of damages which are known as punitive damages. Now, we leave Mike Egan for a minute. I want to spend the remainder of my time talking about punitive damages. I feel this is absolutely the most important aspect of this case. There are going to be several jury instructions on punitive damages. I am going to leave the instructions to the Court, because you will hear what the law is on punitive damages. It is fair to say that it boils down to the proposition that for the sake of an example you can assess punitive damages if you find that the company acted either with malice, and that term will be defined to you by the Judge, or—and I say 'or' and not 'and' or fraud, and those terms will be defined for you by the Judge. The malice and fraud definitions embody a paragraph. Oppression is just one sentence: [reads] 'Oppression' means subjecting a person to cruel and unjust hardship in conscious disregard of his rights.

"Well, you don't even have to look for fraud or malice in this case, although I think both of them are there in abundance. But certainly Mike Egan was subjected to cruel and unjust hardship in conscious disregard of his rights."

Next, I told the jury what I believed their true purpose to be and how important it was for society.

"You know, I don't know if you realize this yet, maybe some of you do, maybe all of you do, there are a lot of times in a person's lifetime, your vote doesn't really mean that much. We all vote and somehow we wonder if the vote ever gets counted. I don't think, unless some of you are lucky enough to be elected as a state representative or something, you will ever vote on anything so significant in your life.

"You twelve people hold the power to make your voices heard, to send a message back to Omaha, and that message is going to be heard in that board of directors' room, and it is going to go to be heard in other boards of directors' rooms, and it is going to get around. There is no doubt in my mind that this verdict, if you speak loud enough, is going to be heard by everybody. By the weekend, everybody will know what happened in this courtroom in Pomona, California. It will be news and it will travel. And it will be read, and it will say to everybody, an example is being set in Pomona, California.

"There have been a few similar cases, but this is the leader. This is Mutual of Omaha. This is not Old Republic or old this or that. That is why this case is so important, not only to society, but to good insurance practices, to people who have been disabled and who will be disabled in the future. Your verdict is going to have a significance."

I was now obliged to talk about punishment. I had to drive

home the fact that the punitive award was not to compensate Mike Egan, but to punish Mutual of Omaha. I knew I would have to give the jury some logical guidelines.

"Let's talk about punishment a little bit. I don't even know if this is punishment. I mean, you can't put an insurance company in jail. Is it punishment to pay back the money you stole over the years?

"You know, it is interesting to me that when somebody like me—if I go into somebody's house and steal some money, I am going to jail, certainly most of us [would]. But when it gets sophisticated and it gets on higher levels, of course, you don't have the power to put anybody in jail, a different standard somehow is applied."

I had to correlate the concept of punishment with an appropriate amount of money.

"When we talk about punishing this corporation, we may be talking about an awful lot of money. Money is relative. Say we are talking about $2,000,000; that is a lot of money. It is not a lot of money if you want to buy a 747—it wouldn't even get you a tail. So it is relative. What's a lot of money? The Judge will tell you, in determining the amount necessary to impose the appropriate punitive effect, if you feel punitive damages should be awarded you are entitled to consider the wealth and assets of the company.

"Let me just give you a few examples. Let's take Mr. Segal, his assets or net worth, he says, are about $10,000 or $20,000. Lets take $10,000. If you punish Mr. Segal $10,000, that wouldn't be punishment, it would be persecution. You're not going to take away the guy's bank account, I don't think that is fair to anybody. However, maybe a $1,000 punishment or at least a $500 might be appropriate: a $1,000, for example, if you assume he has got $10,000 net worth—I am not talking about assets—I am talking about assets and subtracting liabilities, net worth, $1,000 is ten percent of his net worth.

"If you apply the same standard to Mutual of Omaha and take their surplus, whichever figure you want to take—there have been three of them, $200,000,000, $162,000,000, and I think there was one in between, $194,000,000, and ten percent of the lowest one is $16,000,000. That sounds like a lot of money, but you are applying the exact same standard to them as you are to Mr. Segal. What's just for the poor is just for the rich. Everybody is supposed to be guided and judged by the same standards of justice in this country.

"Another way to logically support [your verdict] is on the basis of earnings. We punish people on the basis of earnings all the time. You will see in the financial report that last year they made something like $26,000,000 after taxes, and, boy, the taxes, 10 percent taxes. I would like to pay only 10 percent taxes. And if you look real thoroughly, in that annual report, you will find out how much property tax they paid on the building down on Wilshire Boulevard, it was zero. I would say in a case of this sort maybe a month or two or three of earnings would be appropriate. If you are making eight or nine hundred dollars a month and you get caught stealing, or whatever—swindle, fraud, malice, oppression—we might say a fair punishment would be a couple of month's earnings."

I concluded my summary to the jury with these remarks:

"Their own pledge is to support right principles and oppose bad practices in health and accident insurance. There is nothing in this country at this moment, and I think everybody knows that, that will do more to support right principles and oppose bad practices in health and accident insurance [than a large punitive damage verdict]. There is nothing that the legislature can do or will do that is [more meaningful] than what you people do here in this courtroom. And if it is not meaningful enough, it just is going to be something that they get away with again."

Both of Mutual of Omaha's lawyers were allowed to make closing arguments to the jury. Mr. Wild tried to convince the jury that Mutual of Omaha made some mistakes but there was no intent to defraud Mike Egan. He put it this way:

"I don't know whether any of you ever made a mistake, I know I have. A few. And I look back on some that I made like three or four years ago, and I have made some pretty good ones, but when I think back on them, I wonder how I did it. But when I do think back on it, I know that I wasn't really trying to rip anybody off, or I wasn't trying to hurt anybody like that. And I wasn't trying to injure or oppress anybody. These were mistakes, that's all they were. I regret them now, but that is about all I can do . . . We have heard about the famous corporate crack or whatever it is. We have heard how they goofed, that the mistake should have been picked up in Omaha. And all I can say is that—or can ask, if any of you ever worked with a company wherein the procedures went bad sometimes and somebody goofed and something got fouled up, it is very easy. It happens all the time. You can hardly have a company of any size or group of people of any size where that wouldn't happen in spite of all the procedures."

Mr. Wild's arguments to the jury were quite tame in comparison to Mr. Doutre's. He got up and really took after me as just another one of the plaintiff's attorneys making phony arguments and looking for a pot of gold. Doutre really shocked me as he approached the jury box and tried to divert their attention from all the damaging evidence against Mutual of Omaha by attacking me. I listened intently as he blasted away:

"Let me say one other thing—one thing the plaintiff's attorney didn't tell you is where all this money goes. It doesn't go into a trust fund. It doesn't go to the city or county or wherever a criminal fine goes. In my opinion, I can guarantee that if this money went to the city or the county or even a trust fund to help victims of other catastrophes or whatever, these attorneys wouldn't be getting up and telling what a great public service you have done in awarding punitive damages. Heck, this is the pot of gold. this is the big money. This is the big score. This is why we argue that punitive damages shouldn't be given.

"It's just as plain and simple as that, and I hate to be cynical about it, but that is true. If this went someplace else—if this went to the state or in a trust fund or something, you wouldn't hear a thing about it. They just don't tell you where it goes.

"Okay. Now, there is one other little thing here. Counsel has in his argument and in his questions told you here the chief executive officer, the chairman of the board of Mutual of Omaha, gets this $400,000 a year and the president gets this fabulous amount and, so, you know, you should award these punitive damages because they are sitting back—they're fat cats, and here we are robbing these people down here. Well, in the first place, I looked in the report and the chief executive officer, chairman of the board of Mutual of Omaha, doesn't get $400,000. He gets $125,000 a year. That is no cheese, but that is not $400,000, either. The rest of the money—you can read the report—the rest of that money actually was accrued, past compensation that had been accrued over the years, and he took it that particular year. The president of the company gets $74,000, you can read, and I think one other fellow gets a little over $50,000, and everybody else on the list is down below that. Most of them are around in the $30,000. This isn't really very much for a major corporation.

"But the big question is why is he telling you this, why is he arguing this and has nothing to do with what Mutual of Omaha did or didn't do. It has nothing to do with whether you should award punitive damages. You know, I am very amazed how they can argue these things by—these punitive damages and this sort of thing with a straight face, because here they say, we want you to give a very, very logical judgment and a fair judgment, and then they feed you this junk and what's it designed for? It is designed to prejudice you. You are supposed to sit back there and say, 'Gee, that guy is getting all this money, $400,000 a year, and this other little guy is getting nothing; you know, we should award this other little guy something'; and supposed to get you all excited and just the opposite of what you are supposed to be doing.

"It is like the high school coach, you know, when he is preparing for a game, telling the team that, you know, the other team is a bunch of real sissies or something like they all wear purple underwear or beat their mothers, get out there and hit them. This is all it is designed to do. This is all in the world it can do, because it has no relation to punitive damages. It doesn't even have any relation to how much money is in the corporation. So, it is designed to prejudice you. And 100 percent of all this jazz about the corporate assets is the same thing. We have a great big company with all that money up here, you know, give it to us. Well, it doesn't have that much to do or anything really to do with whether these defendants intended to injure Mr. Egan through defrauding him or through oppressing him. It doesn't have anything to do with that, and it is this latter thing that you have to decide what these people do, did they have this evil motive...But I tell you that this argument—these arguments you have been getting concerning this punishment and this punitive damages against Mutual of Omaha are essentially false, phony arguments. They just—you know, let's get the pot of gold, "Let's get the big score, and that's about it."

Fortunately, the plaintiff gets the last word in closing argument. The court always allows the plaintiff's lawyer a short rebuttal. We had put on a straightforward and sincere case, and I thought it was a big mistake for Mutual's lawyers to attack me. I spoke for only five minutes and started out my rebuttal by stating:

"Ladies and gentlemen, apparently they don't care who they call a phony because I guess that is now what I am supposed to be. They are not very discriminating who they apply that term to or when or how. Interestingly enough, when this case first started, did you hear them one time in opening statement say they were wrong or they made a mistake? Not once. When this case first started, not once [did they say] they were wrong or they made a mistake. They just change with the tide. They are not leveling with you...they never have and they never will until you make them pay attention by your verdict. All they can really think of to defend themselves is to attack me and our motives. Whatever you were going to punish them before these arguments started, I hope you will double it, now that you have seen their true colors."

I finished my rebuttal by reminding the jury what this case was all about. This wasn't a personality contest, this was important business. I had the feeling that every juror realized that this case was going to be significant. I never was more sincere in my life than when I told the jury my last words.

"Nobody is trying to break any company. I certainly wouldn't even suggest that in the least. But we do have a lot of people around that believe very strongly in decent and honest practices in the business, and they are all rooting for you. There are a lot of people that will be sick and disabled in this country in the future and shouldn't be cheated out of their money, they're all rooting for you. And, believe me, ladies and gentlemen, every one of those people [is] counting on you and your good judgment and your sense of basic fairness and decency. And I just pray that someone gives you the power to see what is right and do what is right.

"Thank you very much."

The jury went out and deliberated approximately two days. They awarded Michael Egan $45,600 in past and future benefits under his disability policy, $78,000 for mental and emotional distress, and a record-setting $5 million in punitive damages.

The verdict streaked through the insurance community

and the press. Headlines appeared in dailies nationwide, from the *Los Angeles Times*, "Roofer Awarded $5.1 Million in Suit Against Insurance Firm" to the *Las Vegas, Review Journal*, "Mutual of Omaha Caught in $5.1 Million Judgment." Even the *Cork Examiner*, Mike's hometown paper back in Ireland, told its readers, "Emigrant Makes Legal History."

The Honorable Howard McClain—presiding at the trial—was a seasoned and respected judge of the Los Angeles Superior Court. He also must have been unimpressed by Mutual of Omaha's testimony, because he ruled as a matter of law that the company's conduct reflected bad faith. He refused to grant Mutual a new trial or to reduce the size of the award.

After the trial, I knew my career would center full-time on insurance bad faith cases. For this reason I left the partnership of Hafif and Shernoff and established my own practice in Claremont, concentrating on my new specialty. With public attention focused increasingly on these consumer-oriented cases, more and more aggrieved policyholders approached me to do battle against the insurance industry.

In the meantime, Mutual of Omaha appealed the case all the way to the California Supreme Court. The entire appeal took almost five years, but was worth waiting for. Trial results do not set legal precedents, but Supreme Court decisions do. They hand down legal principles that live on to be the guidelines for future cases. Everyone waited patiently for the Supreme Court to speak. Finally the landmark decision came on August 14, 1979. Many of the legal principles I had hope for were now going to be established law.

The Supreme Court's lengthy opinion started out by warning that insurance companies have a trust relationship with their insureds that encompasses the public interest. When an insurance company takes advantage of this special relationship, public-policy considerations support imposing punitive damages upon the company. The Supreme Court explained it this way:

> "The insurers' obligations are rooted in their status as purveyors of a vital service labeled quasi-public in nature. Suppliers of services affected with a public interest must take the public interest seriously where necessary, placing it before their interest in maximizing gains and limiting disbursements...the obligations of good faith and fair dealing encompass qualities of decency and humanity inherent in the responsibilities of a fiduciary. Insurers hold themselves out as fiduciaries, and with the public trust, must go private responsibility consonant with that trust...the availability of punitive damages is thus compatible with recognition of insurers' underlying public obligations and reflects an attempt to restore balance in the contractual relationship."

Thus the *Egan* case represented a clear expression by a California court that defined the scope of bad faith law. It not only addressed the parties involved in the lawsuit, but now concluded that there was a clear public interest at stake. A private citizen could file a suit to punish insurance companies for behavior that was in violation of public interest in order to protect the consuming public. This guiding legal principle has been adopted by other states as well.

The *Egan* decision was a far reaching decision which touched many aspects of the insurance business. *Egan* was the first Supreme Court decision to hold an insurance company guilty of bad faith if it fails to investigate the policyholder's claim adequately. As you have seen from the *Egan* trial, Mutual did a miserable one-sided job of investigating his claim. The California Supreme Court pointed out:

> "The insured in a contract like the one before us does not seek to obtain a commercial advantage by purchasing the policy—rather, he seeks protection against calamity....The purchase of such insurance is to provide funds during periods, when the ordinary source of the insured's income—his earnings—had stopped. The purchase of such insurance provides peace of mind and security in the event the insured is unable to work....To protect these interests it is essential that an insurer fully inquire into, possible bases that might support the insured's claim."

The court went on to hold squarely that:

> "An insurer cannot reasonably and in good faith deny payments to its insureds without thoroughly investigating the foundation of its denial."

Michael Egan opened the door for consumers and made it easier for them to bring their insurance companies to court. The case helps consumers obtain favorable verdicts not just for their claims, but for damages suffered because of mental distress and for punitive damages. The standard of reasonableness is now applied, and a company's entire investigatory process is held up for scrutiny. Was the investigation adequate? Was it thorough? Above all, was it fair?

The court really pointed out a very simple proposition, one that should have been obvious: insurance companies take premiums from their policyholders to protect them and they ought to act like protectors. For the past 100 years the problem has been that once a person files a claim, he is treated more like an adversary than like someone in need of protection.

During the trial, Mutual of Omaha argued that the corporation could not be punished for the acts of its agents and employees—if those agents were low-level employees who were not part of management. The company maintained that a claims adjuster may do something stupid or even wrong, yet the company should not be punished for his errant behavior.

The Supreme Court disagreed. An insurance corporation is liable for the actions of claim adjusters. The court pointed out that from Egan's standpoint, the actions of the claim adjusters were the actions of Mutual of Omaha. Claim adjusters manage the most crucial aspects of the corporation's relationship with its policyholders. Finally, the court found that Mutual of Omaha should not be allowed to insulate itself from liability by giving an employee a nonmanagerial title and then allowing him to make crucial policy decisions.

As if these rulings did not devastate the insurance industry enough, the decision resulted in yet an other important legal precedent. The court said that policyholders were not limited to damages at the time their cases came to trial, but that they could also receive future damages—such as future benefits payable under the insurance policies or future mental distress, in an amount which the jury determines to be reasonable.

For example, at the time that Egan's case came to trial, his disability insurance policy would only have paid him a couple of thousand dollars up to that date. Yet, if he were to receive the benefits for his entire lifetime, those benefits could reasonably have been calculated at $46,600. The jury found the entire amount due and payable at once because of Mutual of Omaha's bad faith, and awarded the entire $46,000 as well as $78,000 in emotional distress, some of which had been suffered in the past and some which still would be suffered in the future.

After giving Egan and the public at large such a tremendous victory by setting forth great legal precedents, the court handed Mutual of Omaha a bone. It determined that the $5 million in punitive damages was too severe and ordered a retrial on this single issue so that another jury could determine what an appropriate punishment might be. Thus, for Michael Egan, the battle wasn't over after 10 years of fighting. Fortunately, just before the retrial, Mutual of Omaha agreed to a settlement to avoid the second trial. They insisted that the details of the settlement be kept confidential, and the court file was sealed. However, in signing the confidentiality agreement, I modified it to make sure I reserved for myself the right to recount my personal recollections about the case and trial.

The legal precedent created by the *Egan* case lives on and has given much-needed help to those who have followed Egan, by opening up the doors of justice to abused policyholders.

# Chapter 2

# How Much Is a
# $48 Gripe Worth?

Elmer Norman walked into my office one day in 1976 wearing a homemade hearing aid. As the slender elderly man entered, he immediately struck me as appealing and unique. He had made his hearing aid by connecting stereo headphones to a box hooked to his belt. To ask questions, I had to speak through a microphone plugged into Elmer's device. I liked him from the very beginning. He was a most unforgettable character with a $48 gripe.

Elmer's friendly gray-bearded face was filled with compassion and intensity. He wore a striped shirt, a gray sweater-vest and a checkered over-shirt, but he was not concerned with his appearance. He had only one good eye, and it was magnified by thick glasses. As he told his story I knew that even though he was nearly blind and deaf, Elmer had a powerful sense of smell. In this case, he smelled a rat.

Elmer told me now Colonial Penn Franklin took advantage of him by refusing to pay a $48 claim. Spinning out his story with many digressions, Elmer always came back to the central point: the company had cheated him and he had proof. His frustrated story convinced me. Besides the merit of his argument, I knew Elmer's personality would appeal to a jury because he possessed a strange wisdom: one that you could listen to for hours on the Johnny Carson show, for example.

Colonial Penn had refused to pay for Elmer's medicine and a hearing test. Insurance claim adjusters argued that the policy excluded the test as well as Elmer's over-the-counter prescription medicine. Though Colonial Penn conceded eventually that it should have paid for the prescription, the company refused to admit any bad faith in denying Elmer's claim for a hearing test.

I had some doubts about filing a suit over a $48 claim, but I also had a gut feeling about Elmer and about the company. My intuition was confirmed when soon after we filed the original suit, my staff uncovered what we believed was a much grander deception.

I joined Elmer in his $48 battle against the Colonial Penn Franklin Insurance Company. I never dreamed, though that Elmer's case would become one of the greatest David and Goliath legal battles of my career.

My first confrontation with Colonial Penn occurred in the fall of 1978. I had sued the company on behalf of Anne M. Costello, a sixty year-old Santa Monica, California resident. In 1976 the elderly woman had been hospitalized 98 days in Rancho Los Amigos Hospital, in nearby Downey. For 59 of those days, Mrs. Costello occupied the intensive-care ward. Confined in an iron lung, she had suffered acute respiratory problems requiring tracheotomy surgery. Her hospital bill totaled $21,000. Mrs. Costello expected to recover a portion of medical costs under a hospital policy she purchased because she was a member of AARP (The American Association of Retired Persons). At that time Colonial Penn was the only insurance company selling medical and hospital coverage for AARP members.

Colonial Penn denied Mrs. Costello's claims, arguing the Rancho Los Amigos Hospital represented primarily a rehabilitation institution and therefore was an ineligible hospital under the terms of the coverage even though it was accredited as an acute-care hospital. Our suit asked for punitive damages stemming from Colonial Penn's bad faith dealings. We also asked for other damages for Mrs. Costello's mental suffering caused by her bills remaining unpaid.

Between the time I took the *Costello* case and the trial, the relationship between Colonial Penn and AARP had been examined and criticized by numerous groups, at least four state insurance departments (Massachusetts, Illinois, Wisconsin, and Minnesota); the Federal Trade Commission; *Consumer Reports;* "60 Minutes"; the Securities and Exchange Commission, and *Forbes.* Consumer-oriented groups, composed of older people seeking reform within AARP and in its relationship with Colonial Penn, had also criticized the relationship. These examinations spurred several lawsuits by former association employees and by current AARP members. Unfortunately, the numerous investigations and suits criticizing Colonial Penn Group, Inc.'s domination over AARP resulted in little more than wrist slapping.

Colonial Penn and AARP were accused of a sweetheart relationship, rubber-stamping and conspiring to increase membership in order to increase profits. Critics claimed what may have started as a service to retired Americans had been corrupted by greed. Since the early 1960s, *Washington Post* writer Morton Mintz had covered the relationship between Colonial Penn and the association. Mintz also investigated Leonard Davis, who was the founder of Colonial Penn and the moving force behind the cozy relationship. He reported that Davis seemed to be a man "who could turn base metal into gold."

These facts led me to reevaluate Mrs. Costello's claims against Colonial Penn and AARP. Rather than confining my argument to the company's original denial of her legitimate claim (Colonial Penn paid the claim after we filed suit), I decided to emphasize Colonial Penn's domination of AARP. Our trial brief accused AARP of being "nothing more than an elaborately disguised merchandising showcase for Colonial Penn."

To support the charges, I introduced two former AARP executives, Harriet Miller and Francis Seeley. Miller had acted as executive director of AARP from February 1976 until she was fired twenty months later. Her strong testimony confirmed our charges. Seeley, former treasurer of AARP, told the jury that as treasurer the association never allowed him access to its finances or those of Colonial Penn. The former AARP treasurer added that he had no idea how the two organizations made decisions. Although he was treasurer for two years, he never spent more than two days carrying out his duties because nobody ever let him. When Judge Francis X. Marnell allowed these two witnesses' testimony, I believed we had won.

With such encouraging developments, I thought our case represented the first test case questioning Colonial Penn's dominance and control over AARP. But I was wrong. The judge's decisions in the case were highly unusual. First, he admitted the testimony of Miller and Seeley into evidence, and then struck it all and instructed the jury to disregard it. Looking back, I believe he decided we had not pleaded the case broadly enough at the beginning. When we began, the case simply involved an unfair claim decision and nothing else. Now we were trying to show a conspiracy.

The domination/conspiracy issued did not cross our minds until just a short time before we went to trial. Initially I had convinced the judge to let me introduce evidence of a conspiracy; otherwise I would have never been allowed to bring Miller and Seeley all the way from the East Coast. However, when he abruptly changed his mind and threw out their testimony, I think he tainted the jury.

The whole experience was depressing. I truly believed that the myriad charges against Colonial Penn were valid; I felt all along that the trial developed in our favor.

The jury deliberated over a day. The clerk had collected all of our phone numbers and knew where to find me. I was meeting with a "CBS Reports" crew at the Beverly Wilshire Hotel in Beverly Hills, helping correspondent Fred Graham and producer Irina Posner with a documentary called "See You in Court."

I had just walked into the room, shook Graham's hand, and greeted Posner when I was called to the phone. The jury had reached a verdict. The court clerk encouraged me to stay on the phone and let the judge take the verdict; otherwise we would have to delay things until I could rush back to court. I really wanted to be in court, but I knew the judge was impatient and I did not want to hold up the CBS documentary.

In great suspense, I waited for several minutes, phone to my ear. Finally, the clerk returned to the phone and told me the jury had ruled against Mrs. Costello. I was so crushed that I could hardly talk to the CBS people. For weeks Mrs. Costello was confined to intensive care, extremely sick. In court, she had to testify with a respirator strapped to her back. Now the jury had awarded her nothing.

I was too depressed to work. After receiving my phone call, Graham would later recall, I was ashen. I knew Graham and Posner wanted to talk about insurance. Instead, they spent the whole lunch hour trying to prop me up. Graham found it surprising that I wanted to help with the television project in the middle of a trial. After the verdict, he encouraged me to leave, but I stayed, and after lunch we got back to work. Much later he told me he was amazed that I followed through with the TV special after such a blow. I guess it was good therapy.

The letdown stayed with me. I knew Elmer's case presented a different sort of problem, but my feelings were unclear. I wanted it and I did not want it. Although I wanted another chance at Colonial Penn, I knew I could not endure another frustrating experience without better results. Four states and the post office had conducted investigations, concluding that something was fishy, yet there was nothing conclusive on whether or not the company had committed any wrongdoing.

Finally, depression transformed itself into inspiration that made me go ahead with Elmer's case. Court congestion in

California often results in months—sometimes years—of waiting before a trial can be set. Sometimes new facts emerge and often memories fade. As the trial date neared, Colonial Penn attorneys wanted an updated deposition from Elmer. They hoped to reassure themselves that they had missed nothing. The deposition, taken on December 19, 1979, gave them more than they bargained for.

In the deposition, Elmer, rambled on, telling how his prospects for medical security had vanished and describing his various frustrations. Then the dam broke. Suddenly he forgot about his $48 claim and launched into a tirade about his benefits being reduced by a switch in policies. This was news to us and startled everyone. In his rambling manner, Elmer explained:

> "I discovered to my horror and sorrow that I...had been lulled to sleep...Colonial Penn was promising the sun, moon and stars concerning improved benefits...I discovered, though, that in the matter of the out-of-hospital policy that what they promised as being improvements were really reductions in benefits. There was an increased deductible, new limitations on drugs...and a fantastic reduction for 80 percent of the allowable benefits in a certain number of categories down to only 20 percent."

After Elmer's new testimony, the complexion of the case changed even though the significance of the switch in policies was not fully understood at that point. Learning from the *Costello* experience, the deposition made it clear that I needed to broaden Elmer's lawsuit and include the switch in policies. I amended the original documents to incorporate the charge that Colonial Penn had changed the policies fraudulently. That issue would now be the centerpiece of the lawsuit.

Once amended, I filed the complaint, and new discovery proceedings were initiated. I requested from Colonial Penn

copies of all documents relevant to the policy switch. I was
sent 300 pages of material.

Some papers were pure gold. Documents revealed that
Colonial Penn's true intention was to revise the out-of-
hospital coverage in order to reduce loss ratios by 40%. The
policy switch would save the company over $4 million in
payouts per year. Interoffice memos and directives set forth
detailed revisions that would make the new plan appear
similar to the old.

The most damaging company memos were written by
Daniel Gross, president of several of Colonial Penn's
subsidiaries, and Richard Saltzman, then a Colonial Penn
Franklin vice-president.

The Gross memo—sent to company executives on March
29, 1973—summarizes the plan to reduce claims payments
by 40%.

> "We are attempting to reduce claim payments by
> 40%. If continued claim cost inflation continues,
> revision should result in a 72-75% loss ratio in 1974.
> We propose two basic changes which will achieve
> about half of our 40% reduction objective. These
> changes involve reducing the amount paid on
> medical supplies. X-rays and laboratory tests (which
> are paid under Medicare) to 20% of eligible expenses
> and establishing a separate drug deductible."

Saltzman's directive tells the person responsible for
making document changes to proceed with what he refers
to as a total revision of the out-of-hospital plan.

> "This plan is going to be totally revised to
> incorporate certain benefit reductions in lieu of a
> rate increase. This plan will be divided into three
> parts, each having a separate deductible or
> maximum."

Two other documents were equally damaging to Colonial
Penn. These undated and unsigned memos, one
handwritten, explained why the company was doing what

it was doing and what the objectives were.

The handwritten memo read:

"In 1971 the earned premium was $13,432,102 and incurred claims were $12,417,102 which give OOH [out-of-hospital] a 92.4% loss ratio. In order to get a loss ratio of 60% for 1971, claims must be reduced to $8,059,261 which is a 36% reduction in paid claims. If we assume that 1974 claims will have 10% increase as a result of inflation then, claims should approximately be at a 66% level. Therefore our approximate target is $8,000,000. Assuming incidence of claims will not be affected by our changes or by any external factors than we can concentrate on manipulating the aggregate paid claims."

The typewritten list of objectives summarized things nicely:

*Objectives of Revision*

1. *Reduce claims cost by 40%.* [emphasis is author's]

2. Permit elimination of pre-existing condition exclusion.

3. Limit future claim cost inflation.

4. Prevent drug benefit dominance.

5. Minimize variety in coinsurance amounts.

6. *Appear similar to current plan.* [emphasis is author's]

I felt a sense of relief when I saw those papers. We would now be able to show Colonial Penn's actions without delving into the issue of its control over AARP.

My enthusiasm for the case increased. In a gesture of friendship and in an atmosphere of excitement, I invited Richard Ben-Veniste, who had made a tremendous reputation as the Watergate prosecutor, to join me in court. Now in private practice, Ben-Veniste and I had cultivated a friendship for some time. Interested in bad-faith cases, Ben-Veniste was anxious to help me prove one. That was fine with me, except I knew that once you try to set an example, you usually fall flat on your face. But Ben-Veniste became a great boost to me in many ways. He helped with planning and court strategy.

Ben-Veniste was a great help in keeping Elmer on track during the trial's first phase. In one session I had Elmer under direct examination, trying to direct him to tell his story in a chronological and coherent fashion. The task did not come easily since he tended to ramble a bit and stray off the point. I did not mind this occasionally—for it comprised part of Elmer's character. But, if Elmer rambled too much, it would definitely hurt his case. The jury might think he lacked the capacity to think clearly. At one point in his testimony, when his rambling became excessive, I called a recess so I could talk to him.

Elmer remained on the witness stand with his earphones covering his ears. After the courtroom emptied, I picked up the little microphone hanging from his side. Calmly I told him to stick to the point. Simply answer questions without elaborating, I said. Elmer did not understand, he was frustrated, he repeatedly asked me why. With little recess time left, I had not time to explain why. My frustration grew as the seconds ticked by.

Finally, Ben-Veniste grabbed the microphone from me and said to Elmer, "Do you want to know why?" and Elmer nodded his head. Ben-Veniste then raised his voice and shouted into the microphone, "Because unless you stick to the point, you're going to lose the fucking case." I knew he had gotten through when I saw a broad smile return to Elmer's face. From that point on, we had no trouble with rambling.

His unassailable character emerged during the trial's very first day. We had wired Elmer's headphones to the court system so he could hear. As soon as Elmer's direct examination began, his personality lit up the room. Colonial Penn's lawyer was Richard Castle of Los Angeles. The Honorable Arthur Baldonado presided.

Shernoff: "Mr. Norman, can you hear me?" [repeat] Mr. Norman, can you hear me?"

Elmer: "Yes, sir."

Q. "Okay. Can you tell the jury where you live?"

A. "I live in Azusa."

Q. "When were you born?"

A. "New York."

Q. [louder] "When? What year?" I asked what year you were born."

A. "1908."

Q. "Are you comfortable in the chair there, do you want—"

A. "I'm having some difficulty with—"

Q. "Why don't you sit back in the chair? They will bring the mike up to you. Why don't you sit back and relax? Okay. If you can. Are you a little nervous?"

A. "Yes. I feel that I ought to apologize for putting such impediments in the way of the normal proceedings of a normal trial, you know. But I'm sorry, I just can't help it. And I think we will get by with the—"

Q. "What is the extent of your formal education?"

A. "I had several years of university and college. I did not graduate."

Q. "What occupation did you have while you were in New York?"

A. "The chief thing was that I worked with my dad. I became a manager for his drug store in Astoria and the store in Staten Island, too, in New York."

Q. "When did you come to California?"

A. "We came to California in '47."

Q. "Before coming to California, did you have any physical problem with your ear or your eye?"

A. "Before coming to California? Oh, yes. We will start with the ear; that was the first thing. I caught an extremely bad infection, a very virulent streptococcus infection. In those days they didn't have quite as good drugs as we have today. But there was this sulfanilamide, it was relatively new. And it so happened my doctor was quite competent, up-to-date, and he got hold of some of it. He opened my eardrum through surgical procedures and packed the ears with sulfanilamide powder and saved my life.

But the aftermath of that was, as he told me it would be, that I would definitely lose my hearing but at such a very slow stage that I wouldn't notice. And that turned out to be true."

Q. "Any other physical—"

A. "Oh, my eye. I was skating at a skating rink in Baltimore, as part of an amusement enterprise I was managing, and a young kid swung a pair of roller skates with steel wheels and the axle or something hit the lens of my eye, drove a splinter—punctured the eyeball. I lost so much fluid that by the time I was operated on, I lost the sight of the eye. That, of course, was a physical accident, not really an illness."

Q. "After coming to California, what type of work did you do?"

A. "Oh, I worked in management of real estate with my mother and dad. But chiefly I managed an apartment house that my mother had in Arcadia."

Elmer's career did not reveal his true abilities. He had setbacks and disappointments. Managing his parents' modest real estate investments and, in later years, caring for his acutely sick mother, replaced his own career. Elmer's marriage failed, and his wife returned to her homeland, Canada, taking Carol, their seven-year-old daughter with her. The fifteen-year separation from his only child was hard on Elmer. Later, in her early twenties, Carol joined her father in Southern California and completed her degree in library science.

For decades, Elmer had preoccupied himself with politics and social issues. He subscribed faithfully to libraries of up-to-date journals and consumed several daily newspapers voraciously. During our friendship, Elmer would never let an opportunity pass to note the plight of the American consumer. Elmer told the *Los Angeles Times*, "I've always been interested in the consumer. Where is the law that protects us? What can one person do alone?"

A discussion group made up of older citizens like himself was the mainstay of Elmer's social life. He enjoyed playing penny-ante poker with his buddies at the club.

Though by no means a recluse, Elmer's responsibilities and unique interests made him a loner. He thought a great deal about economic injustice and he had felt victimized by common consumer problems. Yet, not until his health-insurance carrier turned down his small claim did Elmer decide to fight the system.

I did not want to focus on the deception from the switch in policies at the beginning of the trial; this issue would come in due time. First I wanted the jury to understand Elmer. I needed the jurors to understand the innocent nature of his relationship with Colonial Penn from the beginning.

Shernoff: "Do you recall approximately when you purchased the Colonial Penn policies that are subject to this case."

Elmer: "When I first purchased it? Oh, yes. In 1967. About October—September or October, November, of 1967. I bought the three policies."

Q. "How did it come about that you heard about these policies?"

A. "I presume that it was due to my mother. She had already been a member of AARP [The American Association of Retired Persons] and was already insured. And she had been a bad, chronic invalid and I used to take care of her accounts. So that is the way I knew about AARP. And the way they knew about me, I presume, was through my connection with my mother, because I handled her accounting with AARP for her.

"Either they put me on the mailing list that way or else I just got it as a matter of advertising, solicitation through the mail."

Elmer was wary of Colonial Penn because his mother had trouble with AARP-related health insurance. Despite his mother's problems with coverage, he separated the insurance carrier and the association mentally. He believed the AARP devoted itself to the well-being of older people. When he joined AARP in 1967, the group was eleven years old and its membership had grown by half a million people per year. In the 1970s, AARP's membership increased dramatically, at the rate of one million per year.

Elmer had no reason to believe that AARP would permit a deception against its membership—certainly not by the insurance company that held AARP's endorsement. The insurance company had an exclusive right to solicit members' business, to advertise in *Modern Maturity*—the association's bimonthly magazine—and to mail its advertising and solicitation letters under AARP's nonprofit mailing status. Colonial Penn had been an integral part of AARP's formation, and AARP had nurtured Colonial Penn. This relationship was a matter of pride to AARP members.

*Modern Maturity* often told senior citizens that before Colonial Penn's founder, Leonard Davis, created group health coverage for AARP members, older American people could not purchase reasonable health and hospital coverage. Elmer thought, as the honorary president of AARP, Davis surely would have the member's welfare foremost in his mind. (Few knew that in twelve years, Davis became one of the richest men in the United States. In 1971 alone, the value of his family's stock increased $60 million. In the first six weeks of 1972, the value of his family stock rose $52.3 million).

Because of his faith in AARP, Elmer bought health insurance from Colonial Penn to supplement his limited Medicare coverage. He assumed that Colonial Penn's foot dragging in his mother's case was endemic to the insurance business. And, if AARP said the health insurance policy was the best buy for several hundred thousand older American citizens, it was bound to be good for him. With this background, I began to discuss his claim.

Shernoff: "Mr. Norman, in 1973—December of that year—do you recall having an ear infection in your inner ear?"

Norman: "73? Yes. About the end—about the middle of December I caught this infection in my ear."

Q. "Do you recall what type of treatment you received for your ear problem?"

A. "Yes. The first thing was to, naturally, examine the ears. So I had a culture test. I had X-rays. I had audio-diagnostic services and prescriptions."

Q. "After you received those services, did you then put in a claim for the payment of those services with Colonial Penn?"

A. "Oh, yes."

Q. "Is that the first time you had a claim under that policy since you purchased it?"

A. "That was my very first claim that I had ever made to the insurance company."

Q. "Did you then, sometime after you put in your claim, receive a benefit check with an explanation of the benefits?"

A. "Yes."

Q. "Do you recall what your reaction was when you first received the benefit check and the explanation of the benefits?"

A. "Well, I was quite surprised because there were several different categories of benefits promised by the policy. I received partial payment only on the drugs. No payment on the audio, on the audio test."

Q. "Did you write a letter to the claims department?"

A. "Yes, then I wrote a letter to the claims department."

The letter, dated April 14, 1974, set forth the number and dates of visits, the treatments, the diagnoses, and the errors Colonial Penn had made in calculating reimbursements.

Shernoff: "After you sent that letter, do you recall getting a response from them?"

Elmer: "Yes, I did."

Q. "Mr. Norman, does this look like the reply you received?"

A. "Yes, shall I read it?"

A. "Yes."

A. "Dear Mr. Norman:

Your letter of April 13, 1974 has been referred to me for reply.

Upon careful review of the claim processed, we find that no additional benefits are due.

The complete audio evaluation performed on December 20, 1973 is considered neither a diagnostic laboratory procedure, nor a diagnostic x-ray procedure, therefore, it cannot be allowed...

Additionally, I found that the correct amount was allowed for prescription drug bills you submitted. According to the 1973 American Druggist's Blue Book the dicloxacillin-Dynapen Capsules are not considered as prescription drugs.

Sincerely yours, Harvey Davis, Claims Department."

Q. "When you received that letter, what was your reaction?"

A. "I felt that they were in error, that they were wrong."

Q. "The letter did state they had made a careful review, is that correct?"

A. "Yes. In other words, they had seen my claim."

From his past pharmacy school days, Elmer recalled that the *American Druggist's Blue Book* cited by Colonial Penn was nothing more than a trade journal. Elmer, all by himself, read federal publications and determined conclusively that a consumer could not buy Dynapen without a prescription—either under its commercial name or the generic designation of dicloxacillin.

Elmer also described what he learned by consulting the *California Relative Studies.* Used by professionals to determine treatment designations and costs, the book had convinced him that his hearing test represented a laboratory procedure. His investigation took several months.

Then I placed in evidence Elmer's next letter to Colonial Penn in which he presented his findings. The letter was dated December 23, 1974. Elmer read Colonial Penn's response—sent a month later—into evidence.

Elmer: "Dear Mr. Norman:
Your letter of December 22, 1974 has been referred to me for reply.

We regret that, through a clerical error your purchase of Dynapen was incorrectly disallowed. Our records are now being corrected and the additional benefits due for the purchase of this drug will reach you shortly...Our decision not to consider hearing or vision tests as laboratory tests is not an arbitrary one. As your letter pointed out, the California Relative Value Study lists tests of this as 'diagnostic procedures', the Out-of-Hospital Medical plan provides benefits for 'Diagnostic laboratory tests.'...

Sincerely yours, Adrienne M. Agnew, Claims Department."

Shernoff: "What was your reaction to this letter when you got it?"

A. "My reaction was very, very definite. Now I was convinced that I was being ripped off. The audio test—the refusal to pay the audio test, that was—that really infuriated me. The whole world, I thought, understood that the test of—diagnostic tests, whether it is in a field of medicine or mining or geology or whatever it may be, does not have—does not have to be a vast sort of laboratory. You can carry a laboratory in your vest pocket."

Elmer explained in greater detail why the hearing test involved a diagnostic laboratory procedure. He enjoyed telling in his homespun manner that the claims staff at Colonial Penn reminded him of the Mad Queen in *Alice in Wonderland* because "they used words to mean whatever they wanted them to."

The $48 claim did not represent the case's major thrust, but I thought it worthwhile to focus the case around a small issue. I wanted the jury to see how Colonial Penn conducted business in this one instance in order to set the stage for the more serious matter: the switch in Elmer's policies.

To present details of the switch, I asked Elmer to read into evidence portions of two letters sent by Colonial Penn—one in the fall of 1973 and one the following January—which dealt specifically with the out-of-hospital health coverage. The letters were addressed to policyholders and explained why the coverage needed revision. The January letter stated in part that the new policy reflected "substantial improvements" in coverage at no additional premium.

The letters did not communicate differences between the original and the new coverage. I intended to show the jury that Colonial Penn wanted the policyholders to believe that they were receiving a bonanza in the new coverage when, in fact, the company was substantially reducing the policy's overall worth. The two letters had been signed by Dorothy Liggett, Coordinator, AARP Insurance Plans.

Shernoff: "What did that mean to you?"

Elmer: "It meant that after the revision, or whatever it was, that I would get an even better policy, that my coverage—my protection would be stronger, higher. My new policy would be better."

Q. "Substantially better?"

A. "Substantially better."

Q. "That is the word they used, right?"

A. "They used the words 'substantial improvements that have been made in your AARP Group Health Insurance.'"

Elmer paid little attention to either letter when he received them, since he assumed that AARP looked after his interests. Elmer took the letters out of his files and reviewed them only after Colonial Penn refused to pay his medical expenses.

As we learned from the corporate memos, when Colonial Penn wrote those letters, its plan was actually to reduce benefits. At the same time, the company and its subsidiaries were amassing one of the quickest fortunes in American corporate history. In 1971 Colonial Penn Group had total revenues of $171 million. Revenues in 1976 totaled $445 million. The AARP health insurance plans alone generated about $261 million in premiums in 1977. In January 1976 the Colonial Penn Group led 929 major United States corporations in profitability, with a five-year average return on capital of 33.5 percent. The figure nearly doubled IBM's or Xerox's profit margins. The 33.5 percent yield tripled the median return of 11.3 percent for the entire insurance industry. Meanwhile, during January 1976, Elmer Norman lived in a modest house supported by Social Security income and dwindling reserves from the sale of his family real estate.

The two Colonial Penn letters would open the door to the jury's view of a deceptive scheme. After realizing what impact the policy switch would have on the jury, I began to feel confident that I now had the key to expose the company's practices. Given the setback I suffered at Colonial Penn's hands and its ability to cleanse itself in the muddiest of waters, I relished this second challenge.

My message to the jury was obvious: Colonial Penn told policyholders it was providing better benefits when, in reality, it was secretly taking them away. The documents proved that. The memos revealed that the revision aimed to reduce claims cost by 40 percent. Worse yet, the way they implemented the goal was to make the new plan appear similar to the old.

The trial lasted fourteen days and produced 1,331 pages of transcript. Of those pages, only 788 covered actual testimony from witnesses before the jury. We spent much court time arguing law, the admissibility of evidence, and the credibility of the six witnesses. The greatest strain on the proceedings, though, involved the case for the defense.

Castle attempted to argue the two critical letters (mailed in mid-1973 and early 1974) were totally unrelated. The first letter, he claimed, informed customers that their previous policies—issued in 1972—would change in November 1973. An additional revision would occur in January 1974. The first letter enclosed a rider, Castle emphasized, which explained the revised coverage. The second letter, he argued, dealt with the company's new decisions, made after the first letter had been mailed. The new decisions described in the second, January letter, were separate and apart from the revisions set forth in the November communications. This was a hypertechnical and confusing defense. It sounded like typical insurance double talk.

The January letter stated there were "substantial improvements" in the coverage. I kept coming back to the fact that I couldn't see any "improvements." There were some added areas of coverage in the new policy but they involved medical costs arising from pregnancy, illness, or injury due to war, care in military or government hospitals, and limited coverage for pre-existing conditions.

I really had fun with this point. I didn't for a second believe they would try to sell the idea to the jury that adding coverage for pregnancy or accidents while in the military would do anything for these old folks. But Castle put on a straight face and tried to defend these additions by noting that nothing prevented an older man from having a wife of childbearing age, although he did concede that such an item did not represent a major risk for the company. The increased risk did not cost the company much. The absurdity of awarding retired people maternity benefits was not lost on the jurors. Some laughed out loud. Castle had little to say about the war-related injuries or veteran's hospital exclusions since, as we pointed out, those hospitals offered free care anyway. Nor did he have much to offer in explaining the elimination of the pre-existing condition exclusion. Having been a long-time policyholder, the new "benefit" would have absolutely no meaning to Elmer or anyone else previously insured.

Howard Clark, a founder of the National Insurance Consumer Organization and former state Insurance Commissioner in South Carolina, testified that the new maternity benefits were "illusionary" and benefits for war and care in military hospitals were "absolutely meaningless."

Concerning Elmer's original complaints—the carrier's refusal to pay for the Dynapen medicine and the audiogram ear test—Castle argued that making a mistake was anyone's province. The company did pay when it discovered the Dynapen error. Castle said, "...that is why they have erasers on pencils...." As for the audiogram, everyone was entitled to his own opinion, and Colonial Penn's argument had more credibility than Elmer's said Castle. Nevertheless, he noted in closing argument, that since a reasonable doubt existed, the company changed its policies regarding hearing tests and paid Elmer the $48.

The defense spent the remaining time attempting to justify Colonial Penn's internal documents. The attorneys tried to exclude evidence of Colonial Penn Group's net worth, hoping to minimize possible punitive damages. The parent company, Colonial Penn Group, owned some dozen subsidiaries including Colonial Penn Franklin. Castle failed on the first count and succeeded only partially on the second.

Castle's struggle first to keep the documents from being admitted as evidence and then to keep parts of the documents from entering the record gave us an opportunity to display a little humorous indignation.

> Castle: "Your Honor, my objection goes to the first fact that he is taking isolated sentences or groups of sentences out of the letter, out of context without—"

> Shernoff: "Your Honor, it is right in front of the jury. For him to stand on picking things out of context is ridiculous."

> Castle: "What is in front of the jury I don't know if the jury can read it; hopefully they can but maybe they cannot."

> Shernoff: "You don't know if they can read, counsel?"

When the handwritten memo was introduced, Castle objected to the document as a whole.

> Castle: "...on the ground that the document, number one does not purport to have an author. Does not purport to have an addressee. It is undated. And there is absolutely no information as to who authored it or if in fact the person who authored it had any authority or managerial capacity within Colonial Penn Franklin to issue such a document ..."

After arguing the same point in several ways, Castle declared that the expert witness on the stand should not be asked to interpret what was going through another person's mind, especially an unknown person.

I countered, arguing that the defense had every opportunity to produce the person who wrote the document. I encouraged the defendants to let that mystery person speak for himself. After all, Colonial Penn had given me the document. "If they want to explain it away," I suggested, "then say it was some shoe clerk that did it, let them bring in the shoe clerk..."

The argument over the document, out of the presence of the jury, takes up eleven pages of testimony. The judge ruled in our favor after the final exchange, specifically over the phrase "concentrating on manipulating the aggregate paid claims." Castle wanted that phrase kept out of the evidence.

Castle's repeated attempts to prevent admission of the documents failed and the trial drew to a close. Castle decided to pursue a new tactic. Even if the documents did say what they said and they meant what they said, surely they did not intend to deceive. Instead, the documents tried innocently to provide the best solution for thousands of elderly citizens. In his closing argument, Castle tried to convince the jury in this way.

> "But if in fact Colonial Penn Franklin was devious, fraudulent, was dishonest, you would never have seen those documents, ladies and gentlemen... Now, if there were any documents that looked bad, Colonial Penn Franklin could have destroyed the document or just not produced them. There is no way Mr. Shernoff would know, no way you would know. These are the documents that come out of the bowels of the old records of Colonial Penn Franklin."

The implication that it is easy and probably common for litigants to break the laws of discovery when it suits them is certainly a strange argument for a lawyer attempting to defend his client's honor in a closing argument. I handled that point in the following way:

"How silly. How silly. How dumb does he think people are? We are in a lawsuit now. When you are talking about producing documents in a lawsuit and you do something wrong in a lawsuit or you lie under oath, that is perjury. And if you don't produce something that is supposed to be produced in a lawsuit, you can be held in contempt of court.

"And look at all the important people on these documents. The president of the company, all these executives. Now, they may not be too concerned about turning over, documents [that could lead to] a punitive damage award. But if they don't turn over documents, and somebody finds out about it later, they go down the road to the other country club, the one that has got bars on it. That is why we got those documents. Those important people didn't want to run the risk of not turning them over, and I don't blame them."

Having failed to keep the damaging memos out of evidence, Castle's next effort was to minimize Colonial Penn Franklin's wealth and to suppress all information about Colonial Penn Group's profits. The court compromised on the issue, refusing to allow us to present to the jury the parent company's net worth. We were permitted to enter testimony that revealed Colonial Penn Franklin's profits, generated by health insurance, and how the company funneled those profits up to Colonial Penn Group.

Castle used Robert Saltzman, then executive vice-president of Colonial Penn Franklin and an officer of Colonial Penn Group to rationalize the revisions. Directed by Castle's questions, Saltzman testified that Colonial Penn Franklin was losing money on the out-of-hospital plan. In

1973 that health plan, noted Saltzman, experienced a loss ratio of 100.7 percent. The combined loss ratio of all the health plans totaled 64.8 percent, said Saltzman. The expense ratio (the cost of doing business) for the out-of-hospital plan represented about 30 percent, also higher than for the combined plans, Saltzman added. With a total loss ratio of over 130 percent, Colonial Penn Franklin "lost" over $4 million on the plan. Therefore, the net income for Colonial Penn Franklin in 1973, according to the company's financial statement, was only $1.5 million.

In our cross-examination, we refuted Saltzman's testimony and proved that the company's profits on health insurance totaled nearly $26 million. Colonial Penn's financial manipulation among the group's companies created an illusion that profits were low. I asked Saltzman, according to the 1973 annual statement, the exact nature of the company's pretax income generated by all the AARP-related health plans for 1973. Saltzman gave this answer:

> "Okay, if—I mean—I'm not sure that I can answer that question, but let me try. The $26.6 million is profit on all health insurance business. If we were to subtract from that an estimate of the profit [on certain non-AARP related policies] we would subtract $6.5 million...

> "That would leave roughly $20,000,000, roughly. From that you would have to subtract [certain deferred expenses] of another $2.2 million. So you'd be down to about $17.9 million.

> "And then on that you'd have to subtract something, about $2.6 million, for federal income tax on the remainder. And so I think you'd be down to approximately $13.9 million as the net profit on the AARP Health Insurance Program, as an estimate."

This testimony, which contradicted Saltzman's original estimate of Colonial Penn Franklin's profits ($1.5 million), came only after most precise questioning about insurance accounting procedures in general and about Colonial Penn Group's practices specifically. We showed that the company not only generated a handsome profit from all the health plans, but that the profits increased steadily. Under those circumstances, we asked, why should the company feel it was necessary to change the one policy, when it was doing so well overall?

We based our closing argument on ordinary logic. It helped return Elmer to the jury's consciousness. I stressed how Colonial Penn had repeatedly discounted his claims. First they searched a book under the general name of a drug, and when the book explicitly said, "look under the brand name," they didn't do it. Instead, the company said that the drug wasn't listed as a prescription drug. That's tantamount, I said, to looking in the Yellow Pages for a lawyer and then deciding none existed in your area because under "lawyers" the book says "See Attorneys."

I had to explain the significance of those words "appear similar to current plan." I was eager, but I also had to avoid the evangelism that sometimes overcomes closing argument.

> "Those words are plain English. You don't have to be a Philadelphia lawyer to figure out what they mean ...In other words, let's give it an appearance that is similar. This doesn't say 'let's make it similar.' The word 'appear' is in front of 'similar.' You know, to 'appear' has got a meaning common to all of us. You appear to be what you are not."

Castle contended that it would have been misleading had Colonial Penn told its customers that 40 percent of the benefits were being taken away because this wasn't true for everyone: some would lose more and some less. My response was:

> "If the insurance company couldn't find a way to

tell the truth, it is a sad state of affairs as far as insurance practices [go]. They don't have to say it is going to be exactly a 40 percent reduction. All they have to do is be fair. Disclose. They could say something like "the plan is going to be revised and in the aggregate it is going to be a 40 percent reduction; some people might get more, some people might get less but on the average it will be 40 percent.

"...This company has become one of the most profitable insurance companies in this country [by] riding on the backs of elderly people. They ought to be ashamed of themselves.

"I believe in a decent profit. But I don't believe in an excessive profit, especially when you're dealing with old folks.

"I believe in telling them the truth, the whole truth, not half the truth and not making a bunch of explanations why you can't tell the truth.

"It is up to you, ladies and gentlemen, in the last analysis you are the ones that are going to decide, did they play fair with these elderly people?"

I reminded the jury of those two letters to illustrate just how Colonial Penn Franklin did business with AARP.

"They have [the letters] signed by Dorothy Liggett, Coordinator of AARP Insurance Plans. We know that she has no connection with AARP whatsoever. She is not even a member of AARP. She works as a full-time employee from National Association Plans, which is a wholly owned subsidiary of Colonial Penn Group, which owns the company involved in this lawsuit.

"Now if you get a letter from AARP Insurance Plans, with the AARP seal, signed by Dorothy

Liggett, Coordinator of AARP Insurance plans, do you think you have the right to conclude that maybe this letter is coming from AARP and they knew of this letter and approved of what was going on?"

Testimony during trial, I pointed out, proved that Liggett had nothing to do with the decision to revise the insurance plan. She also had no idea why the company made the revisions. I reminded the jury that AARP Insurance Plans was a non-existent entity, nothing more than a letterhead.

Liggett's deposition testimony showed that she and her title were tools for Colonial Penn.

Shernoff: "As I understand it, you had nothing to do with the preparation of these form letters?

Liggett: "That's right."

Shernoff: "And your signature then was placed [by stamp] on the form letter which went out to the various insureds. Is that correct?"

Liggett: "That's correct."

Shernoff: "Were you told at the time or about the time that your signature was affixed to these letters that the purpose of the change in the Out-of-Hospital Plan was to reduce payouts by 40 percent?"

Liggett: "No, I wasn't."

I ended my argument by explaining the value of punitive damage awards and the several ways these awards can be viewed. Was it punishment at all, in fact, just to take back the money, the ill-gotten gains, that didn't belong to the company to begin with?

"When we talk about punishment in cases involving fraud, malice and oppression, all we are really talking about is a fine, a penalty. Ask yourself what would happen to an individual who...doesn't wear a nice suit, he doesn't make $100,000 a year. He doesn't sit at a country club worrying about his stock options. A man in blue jeans out on the street who decides to defraud somebody. It's not $4.5 million, but let's say, it's $4,000. He gets caught. What happens to him?"

I told the jury that what Colonial Penn understood best was money.

"[Let's] send them a legal message that has a dollar sign on it and tell them "This isn't the way you treat elderly people. If you're going to sell insurance to old people and you're going to make millions and millions of dollars, year after year, you better be fair to them. Because if you're not fair and you start to cut corners, and you [commit] fraud, an American jury is going to tell you to watch your step!"

Castle's closing argument concentrated on absolving Colonial Penn Franklin from charges of malice, fraud, and oppression and on minimizing the company's profits.

The testimony portion of the trial ended at 4:35 P.M. on Friday, November 14. Judge Baldonado told the jury:

"We will reconvene Monday morning at 9:30, at which time I will read the final instructions in the case and then you commence your deliberations. I think it is too late in the day...to hear my boring voice read those things to you. Good night, have a nice weekend."

Meanwhile, Elmer, who had attended most sessions of the trial, stayed away that Monday, November 17. I told him we would call when the verdict came in.

Tuesday morning there was a verdict, and I called Elmer just before I left Claremont for the courthouse. Elmer's car broke down twice on the way from Azusa to Pomona. At 10:20 A.M. the proceedings began, even though Elmer was stranded on the freeway.

> The Court: "In the case of Norman versus Colonial Penn. Mr. Noble [the jury foreman], I understand the jury has reached a verdict."
>
> The Foreman: "Yes, they have, your Honor."
>
> The Court: "Will you hand it to the bailiff. The record will reflect the presence of counsel and the jury panel and the alternate."
>
> "All right, the clerk will read the verdict."
>
> The Clerk: We the jury in the above-entitled action, find for the plaintiff, Elmer Norman, and against the defendant, Colonial Penn Franklin Insurance Company and assess damages as follows:
>
> Compensatory damages, $70,000.
> Punitive damages, $4,500,000."

All the blood drained from Castle's face when the verdict was read. At his request, the court polled the jury. The verdict was unanimous. Castle was always a gentleman, and I remember him as being very gracious. He talked to the jurors and asked them what had gone wrong, and then he made a gentlemanly exit.

About that time, Elmer arrived at the courthouse. He remembers it this way:

> "I came into the courthouse and everybody was still there. The outstanding thing in my mind is how Bill turned around and spied me and he took my hand and shook it and he smiled. I couldn't understand what was happening—as it is, I'm not always in

command of my senses and not always alert, but then I hear him say I won and the verdict was four-and-a-half-million dollars. I was stunned. I went out into the hallway and there was all this buzzing and talking. I started to thank the jurors for giving the case such attention and then the amazing thing was that they thanked me for bringing it to their attention. I remember Castle talking to the jurors. I think he was just flabbergasted."

After battling this giant company again and winning, I remember feeling almost hollow. I wished we were in the middle of the Rose Bowl, with thousands of people around to watch this vindication and see good things happen to this old man.

Elmer Norman still lives in the same jam-packed, memory-filled house. The place is full of his favorite clutter, documents, and gadgetry for electronic tinkering. He is still thinking about moving. He continues to read the papers and plays penny-ante poker. He shares his money with seven relatives, to whom he gives the maximum the law allows. He says it makes him feel good to do that.

Ben-Veniste caught the "bad faith" bug from this case, and we opened a Washington, D.C. partnership to handle insurance bad-faith cases on the East Coast.

Perhaps more than any other case, the verdict demonstrated that no matter how small or infirm a person is, our system of justice allows anyone to make a difference —if he or she is right, and if he or she is persistent. Thanks to Elmer Norman, insurance companies *should* now think long and hard about taking advantage of older policyholders.

Unfortunately, Colonial Penn Franklin did not learn a good lesson by this case. I recently had another tangle with them which resulted in a jury assessing a punitive damage award of $4 million against them. This case involved hospital indemnity policies that we all see advertised on TV. It pays so much a day for every day one is hospitalized. My client, Julius Warren, was hospitalized for approximately 400 days, in a Veterans Administration hospital, after being severely injured in an auto accident. He was completely bedridden, had over 40 broken bones. It took this entire time of hospitalization just to get him back on his feet again. Colonial Penn Franklin only paid for 40 days of this hospitalization, rather than the 400 days. They claimed the balance of the hospitalization was not medically necessary. Colonial Penn Franklin made this decision without consulting the treating physician or examining Mr. Warren. A registered nurse at their home office simply looked at a portion of the hospital records and decided that most of the hospitalization was not medically necessary. They used a definition of "medically necessary" that we believed was different from the definition contained within the insurance policy. The jury awarded Mr. Warren his insurance policy benefits, which amounted to $102,000, and also assessed Colonial Penn Franklin the huge punitive damage penalty. The trial judge upheld the verdict and it is now moving on to the appeal stage.

The point of this case is that people should be very suspect of the hospital indemnity policies that are advertised on TV, sometimes by movie stars. One has to be able to understand the fine print because there are many traps for the unsuspecting. For example, many times skilled nursing facilities, rehabilitation facilities, convalescent homes, extended-care facilities, and other related entities, are excluded from the definition of "hospital." Therefore, it sounds like you may get a lot of money for every day you are in the hospital but, in most cases, people are in an acute hospital for only a short period of time then transferred to other facilities. Under many policies, once this transfer takes place, you don't get paid anymore because it does not meet the definition of "hospital." Also, as in the Warren case, it is important who is going to make the decision of whether a hospitalization is medically necessary. If that decision is left to the insurance company, they may cut you off a lot sooner, even though your treating physician feels that hospitalization is necessary.

The Warren verdict was one of the first cases to attack the abuses inherent in the hospital indemnity policy. These policies are generally sold to the elderly as Medi Care supplements.

These cases point to one inescapable conclusion. The elderly who buy this type of insurance must be very careful to know what they are buying. Stay away from insurance companies and policies which do not deliver what the advertising implies is being sold.

# Chapter 3

# Fighting the Blues

For a lot of people, fighting the blues means suing Blue Shield and Blue Cross to get their medical bills paid. In many of these cases, we've been able to win significant victories for embattled Blues policyholders. Although the amounts of the claims may have been relatively minor, the legal issues are major, and we believe the legal battles may help to change what is a serious flaw in Blue Shield, Blue Cross health plans.

Most Blue Cross and Blue Shield policyholders don't know that even if their doctor orders hospitalization, medical advisers hired by these companies may decide after the fact that the doctors were wrong. When this happens, hospital patients whose conditions appeared life-threatening to their doctor at the time of treatment may come away from the hospital with a clean bill of health and a huge bill for services rendered.

John Sarchett and Barbara Visconti are two people who slugged it out with the Blues. Their stories are typical yet startling examples of the Monday-morning quarterbacking that goes on in Blue health-plan huddles. It's a kind of second-guessing that the policyholder has little chance to discover since there is usually nothing written in the insurance policy explaining this procedure, commonly referred to as "retrospective review." Policyholders are not told their doctor-ordered care is subject to later review by the plans' doctors and administrators.

John Sarchett had been a healthy individual most of his

fifty-seven years. Considered by his doctors as robust and strong, Sarchett rarely missed a day as director of the Los Angeles County Probation Department. One day in 1976, John began having severe stomach and mid-back pain. Several weeks went by before general weakness brought John to Dr. Bruce Van Vranken, his family physician. Dr. Van Vranken examined him but made no diagnosis. He ran some tests and asked John to return if things took a turn for the worse. John went back to his doctor a few days later. Dr. Van Vranken, who described John as looking like "death warmed over," became concerned over what he feared was a life-threatening condition. He ordered John to check in at Foothill Presbyterian Hospital in Glendora, California. Tests were run while nurses and doctors attended to John and tried to relieve his pain. The tests proved negative, except for a finding of anemia and a low white blood cell count. John spent three days in the hospital before his condition improved enough for him to go home. Dr. Van Vranken concluded that John's problem may have been a small bleeding ulcer which simply stopped bleeding.

Eventually John received a $1,116 bill from the hospital; a bill that he had expected his Blue Shield health plan to pay. Blue Shield refused to pay, claiming that John's hospitalization was not medically necessary. Blue Shield administrators had simply overruled the judgment of the attending physician without ever examining the patient. They said they reviewed the hospital records and, in their opinion, John should have been treated as an outpatient. John was left holding the bag, punished for obeying his doctor's orders.

The key question in the case of *John Sarchett* v. *Blue Shield* is: who should make the determination that hospitalization is necessary? John Sarchett said it should be his treating doctor. Blue Shield maintains adamantly that it has the right to make retrospective review of hospital records and reverse the treating doctor's findings.

The scenario was familiar to me, and I knew it was familiar to a significant number of Blue Shield policyholders. I also knew that it would take a court case to change Blue Shield's procedures. We took John's case, hoping that a victory would force Blue Shield to change its ways. Certainly a trial would bring public attention to this vital issue.

In order to resolve the issues quickly, we agreed to arbitrate the matter with Blue Shield. The American Arbitration Association handled the case. At the hearing we presented our evidence, including letters exchanged between Dr. Van Vranken, Blue Shield, and John Sarchett. A key letter for the case was written by Dr. Van Vranken to Blue Shield. It said:

"It is my understanding that Mr. Sarchett was denied coverage for hospitalization. I am writing this letter to strongly protest this action because it is my sincere belief that this hospitalization was completely justified and indeed urgently needed. This patient was seen in my office the day of his hospitalization feeling very weak with a very marked anemia and many other symptoms which in my mind were indeed in need of immediate care.

"In view of the above medical indications, he was subsequently hospitalized at Foothill Presbyterian Hospital. At the time we were very concerned about acute upper G. I. [gastrointestinal] bleeding and even a possible leukemia. He had a great deal of acute upper abdominal distention and distress and we were not sure just what he indeed did have but were concerned that he did have an acute gastrointestinal hemorrhage. It is my sincere professional opinion that immediate hospitalization was indicated for the patient's treatment and welfare as well as for further diagnostic evaluation.

It is my contention that I would have been professionally negligent if I had failed to initiate the above medical procedures as I did. I strongly protest the action of denying his claims and beseech you to grant his hospitalization as he has requested.

"This man is an extremely conscientious person and one who has never abused any insurance [company] or other health care [provider] in the past. Certainly in view of the seriousness of the problem at the time even though it has turned out to be with hindsight not as serious as we indeed thought it was then, I think it is a gross miscarriage of justice not to comply and grant his hospital care. Please contact me if any further questions regarding this patient's care is needed."

We also called Dr. Jack Japenga, the head of the Foothill Presbyterian Hospital Utilization Review Committee, a standard hospital committee that reviews admissions and other hospital procedures. Dr. Japenga told the arbitrator that the hospital committee found John Sarchett's admission fully justified.

Blue Shield's primary defense was based upon its own doctors' hindsight review of John's hospital charts. Testifying for Blue Shield was Dr. Robert Wolf, a retired physician hired by the insurance plan to review medical charts in order to determine questions of medical necessity. Throughout the hearing, Wolf maintained that John's hospital admission was unjustified.

On June 4, 1979, three years after the disputed hospitalization, the arbitrator ordered Blue Shield to pay the $1,116 hospital bill and awarded John $12,000 in damages for mental and emotional distress. Most significant, the arbitrator ordered Blue Shield to pay $300,000 in *punitive damages*. The $313,116 verdict represented a tremendous victory for John and for others who had similar conflicts with the Blues.

The award received immediate public attention from the media. On July 19, 1979, the *Los Angeles Times* reporting on *Sarchett* decision said,

> "Some patients and physicians who have been involved in prior denials of payment by insurance companies see the surprisingly high punitive damages award as victory against what one physician called 'recalcitrant insurance companies who make arbitrary decisions based on hindsight.'"

Blue Shield attorneys told the *Times:*

> "They feared the decision would cause insurers to pull back in their efforts to cut health care costs by screening claims closely and denying unnecessary hospitalizations."

Doctors told the *Times* they hailed the victory:

> "Many private physicians resent what they see as interference with their practice and with the doctor-patient relationship, as well as a questioning of their medical competence when an insurance company denies a claim....They insist that they are in a better position to determine whether a particular patient requires hospitalization than is an employee of an insurance company who has never seen the patient."

It was clear to me that the patient is an innocent victim in Blue Shield's running battle to curb costs and limit overutilizing doctors. I told the *Times:*

> "If Blue Shield has a beef with the doctor or a hospital, the penalty should be against the doctor or the hospital, not the patient."

Usually an arbitration award ends the matter quickly because they are rarely appealed. However, Blue Shield was not going to take this award lying down. It would either have to revamp its entire method of claims review or risk a punitive-damage award whenever a claim was denied based on hindsight. Blue Shield decided to attack the punitive damage award. The arbitration award was set aside by a trial court on a technicality because Blue Shield argued that it had been denied the right to call a second doctor to testify during the aribtration hearing.

I thought the decision to throw out the arbitration was wrong. Additional medical information would have made no difference; another Blue Shield doctor simply would have echoed Dr. Wolf's testimony. We were left with only one thing to do; try the case all over again. This time I wanted it in front of a jury while Blue Shield wanted another arbitration. We were successful, and the stage was set for a jury trial.

My strategy was to present the court with a very strong trial memorandum. I wanted the judge to understand that significant public-interest issues were involved and to support the importance of the punitive-damage aspect. Large punitive awards have a direct bearing on the public because they cause big companies to modify their behavior.

We also wanted to make clear to the judge that we thought Blue Shield would try to confuse the issues and would base its case on medical testimony gathered from an after-the-fact review of hospital records. The testimony would, of course, conclude that the hospitalization was unnecessary. This was not the issue. We knew there could be a difference of opinion; anyone can find doctors who will disagree. Blue Shield hired doctors to conduct a hindsight review of a hospital chart for the sole purpose of reducing claims expense and not to treat patients on-the-spot for their physical suffering. The major and most significant issue was whether Dr. Van Vranken had the right to order the hospital admission based on his on-the-spot analysis of John's condition.

On the day of trial we handed the court our lengthy trial document setting forth our positions. We said, in part:

"There can be no question of the *significant public interest* in this controversy which involves the claims practices of a health insurer which professes to protect literally hundreds of thousands of our citizens against financial hardship resulting from health problems.

"The central issue in this case *is not* whether, based on hindsight, John Sarchett should or should not have been hospitalized. Such an issue certainly would be the subject of varied and different medical opinions. This is a *fallacious* issue that Blue Shield will play on in the hope of shrouding the real issue in this case, to which Blue Shield has no defense.

"Blue Shield will offer no defense to nonpayment of the hospital bill other than to blame the treating doctor, who in this case is a Blue Shield member doctor of some 20 years good standing with an unblemished medical record and a fine reputation in this community.

"This case will decide whether Blue Shield's practice, as described herein, violates its duty of good faith and fair dealing owed to its policyholder. The resolution of this case will have a tremendous impact on thousands of other policyholders who find themselves in similar situations."

The case was tried in front of a jury with the Honorable William McVittie presiding. He was a newly appointed judge whose good reputation preceded him. A former member of the California legislature, he was well acquainted with public policy issues. My opponent was Bill Sturgeon, a good, tough lawyer whom I had faced before in court. We had received a large punitive-damage verdict against Blue

Shield in an earlier case, when Blue Shield refused to pay for a stomach bypass. I knew Sturgeon would be even harder to beat this time around. To make it a little bit tougher, he brought along Tom French, the lawyer who handled the arbitration hearing. Sturgeon called Tom French his "brains."

We presented our case first, as is customary in civil actions. John, the patient, was the first witness. He was articulate and impressive. His wife Evelyn, a registered nurse testified next and she gave a good account of the concern she had for her husband when he became sick in 1976. Dr. Van Vranken also proved an impressive witness. A respected member of the Glendora community and a general practitioner for thirty-five years, Van Vranken had been a member physician of Blue Shield for twenty years. During that time the health plan had never questioned his medical competence.

We also called two doctors from Foothill Presbyterian's utilization review committee. Drs. Jack Japenga and John Camp testified that their committee had reviewed the records thoroughly and had concluded repeatedly that John Sarchett's hospital admission was justified. They told the jury that they had written to Blue Shield of their decision several times.

Our testimony ended with the appearance of Dr. Edward Zalta. Dr. Zalta was then president of the Southern California Physicians Council and a former president of the Los Angeles County Medical Association. We believed that his testimony would reflect the overwhelming sentiment of most of the doctors in Southern California. What he said reinforced what we had been saying all along.

Shernoff: "Do you have an opinion of the adequacy of Blue Shield's review at that time?"

Zalta: "Yes, sir, I do."

Q. "What is your opinion?"

A. "My opinion is that this type of review would be very unfair to the patient, be very unfair to the physician who is responsible for admitting the patient to the hospital, and did no more than satisfy the self-interest of the insurance company, Blue Shield."

Blue Shield's review was based on the hospital chart alone, and not on the doctor's office chart. Blue Shield had not contacted Dr. Van Vranken before it decided to refuse payment. Blue Shield did not know John's medical history. I questioned Dr. Zalta:

Shernoff: "What is your opinion?"

Zalta: "My opinion is that it is impossible to do justice to any review of a hospitalization unless one has first contacted and ascertained from the treating physician his reasons for hospitalization."

I then pursued what Blue Shield did after its initial refusal to pay John's hospital bill. To begin with, the company received a comprehensive letter from Dr. Van Vranken. He explained why he had ordered John's hospital admission. Blue Shield stuck to its guns. I questioned Dr. Zalta about that.

Shernoff: "Now, on the second review on June 23, 1976, Dr. Van Vranken's letter had been received, can you tell us if you have an opinion as to the second review."

Zalta: "Yes, sir, I do."

Q. "What is your opinion?"

A. "I felt that that review, after having

received Dr. Van Vranken's thorough letter, in which he stated in detail the reason for hospitalization, was extremely unfair to the patient because they again denied reimbursement for a justified hospitalization."

Q. "Did you see any reasons in the record for disbelieving Dr. Van Vranken's impressions?"

A. "No, sir, I did not."

I asked Dr. Zalta his opinion of Blue Shield's general practice of retrospective chart review to deny claims.

Shernoff: "And what is your opinion of the retrospective chart review?"

Zalta: "I consider retrospective chart review, which means going back after the fact and trying to reconstruct what happened on an admission some time before, as being extremely inadequate at best. [It punishes] the patient [and is] unfair to the physician because you are using something after the fact, what we call in retrospect. In other words, it is hindsight to see what his thinking was at the particular time, and I feel that in almost all cases it is self-serving to the insurance company."

Later on in his testimony, Dr. Zalta expressed it even more strongly.

Shernoff: "Doctor, what is your opinion of Blue Shield's review process in this case?"

Zalta: "In my opinion, this demonstrates a conscious disregard for patient welfare."

Here was the former president of the Los Angeles County Medical Association, current president of the Southern California Physician's Council, testifying under oath that in his opinion Blue Shield's review process demonstrated a conscious disregard of patient welfare. After this testimony, it must have been clear to the jury that it wasn't just John Sarchett who was upset with Blue Shield, it was most of the medical community.

After we rested our case, Blue Shield stuck to the game plan I had predicted. They called a seemingly endless series of doctors to buttress their decision that John Sarchett's hospitalization was unnecessary. Dr. Robert Wolf testified, as he had at the arbitration hearing. Wolf said, based upon a review of the hospital chart, John's hospitalization was not necessary.

However, I made some headway with Blue Shield's doctors when I focused their attention on the real issue. I cross-examined one of their consulting experts, Dr. Raymond Kieleen, this way:

> Shernoff: "Is it your opinion that on January 13, 1976, when Dr. Van Vranken decided to hospitalize the patient, that Dr. Van Vranken was practicing below the standard of the community?"

> Kieleen: "No, I do not believe that."

> Q. "So, then do you believe that when Dr. Van Vranken hospitalized this patient, that he was practicing medicine well within the standard of medicine in the community?"

> A. "Yes, I do."

> Q. "In the practice of medicine, Doctor, in your opinion, who makes the determination of whether a patient

should be hospitalized?"

A. "The doctor."

Q. "Is that the way it should be?"

A. "Yes."

After both sides were finished, I decided to ask the court to rule, as a matter of law, that Blue Shield violated its duty of good faith and fair dealing. Factual determinations—the what-who-when-where questions—are for the jury to determine, but legal determinations—those questions where the law applies to undisputed facts—are for the judge. The question of who has the right to determine whether a patient should be hospitalized appeared to me to be a legal matter. I felt most strongly that the answer had to be the treating doctor. It was simple logic that the person best able to treat the patient was the doctor who examined him. I thought that the only way Blue Shield could reserve the right to second-guess the treating doctor would be to write such a provision in their policies; and I knew, as did everyone else, that there was no such provision in the policy. Blue Shield wouldn't want such language in their policies; otherwise it would not be able to sell them.

After hearing arguments and reviewing legal authorities, Judge McVittie made the following ruling:

> "Most people who have such health insurance coverage would assume that they are required to rely on the judgment of their physician when they go to the hospital.

> "I note that when Blue Shield advertises, they point out a feature of their plan is the choice of member physicians, yet nowhere in a Blue Shield brochure is it pointed out to a potential subscriber or present subscriber that those who choose the plan may not rely on their own physician's judgment in determining whether or not their coverage applies.

"In the instant case there is a classical case of conflicting medical judgment: the judgment of Dr. Van Vranken versus that of Dr. Wolf. The decision was resolved here by Blue Shield in favor of its own economic interests to the detriment of the interest of its insured.

"I appreciate the fact that an organization such as Blue Shield must control its costs, but the costs of the plan should not be kept competitive with other plans through denial of benefits that are expected, and this type of practice only promotes the continued deception of the public where they are called upon to make a critical choice between competing health plans. Therefore, as a matter of law, the practice of Blue Shield in disagreeing with the judgment of the treating physician to hospitalize his patient solely on the basis of retrospective review of hospital files is found to be a violation of the duty of good faith and fair dealing."

This was a great legal victory. The only remaining question for the jury would be the matter of damages. The court's ruling did not entitle us automatically to punitive damages. The standard for awarding punitive damages is more rigid than the standard for determining bad faith. I would have to convince the jury that Blue Shield disregarded John Sarchett's rights consciously. The thrust of my argument was simple:

"We must put two things in perspective. Here is Dr. Van Vranken. He actually sees the patient. He knew this person for a long time. [John] was always healthy. He saw [John] a week before in the office. He examined him. He knew the patient. In Dr. Van Vranken's view, [John] was slowly losing blood; he was worried about acute bleeding. He knew the patient had some swelling or distention. He knew the patient was in pain.

"Basically, Dr. Van Vranken, a very good doctor in the Glendora community, thought [John] looked like death warmed over and he thought his patient was dying. He thought his patient was dying and he did what a good doctor should do; put him in the hospital and find out what's wrong with him. Dr. Van Vranken thought he would have been guilty of malpractice had he not done that, and I agree with him.

"If John Sarchett went home and bled to death, there would probably be grounds for malpractice, so he put him in the hospital to see what was wrong with him. Maybe he didn't do every test Blue Shield would have liked, or maybe he didn't order everything that Blue Shield would have liked to see, but basically he put his patient in the hospital because he thought he was sufficiently sick to be in the hospital. Look at what Blue Shield did in this case.

"Dr. Wolf did not see the patient, did not talk to the doctor, did not consult with the doctor, only looked at the hospital records, only looked at the chart, and he made a decision on March 19, 1976, that the patient wasn't sufficiently ill to be in the hospital. Now, that's what we say is a conscious disregard of the patient's rights."

I took about forty-five minutes to argue the case. Then Sturgeon got up and talked to the jury for over an hour. He went over each piece of correspondence, all of the hospital charts, all the testimony laboriously, in an obvious attempt to have the jury turn its attention away from the main point. Sturgeon wanted to demonstrate to the jury that Blue Shield's review was the best they could do under the circumstances. He closed his argument this way:

"I suggest to you that punitive damages in this particular case are unwarranted and would be excessive. I truly believe and hope that corporations such as Blue Shield will get the same kind of determination that you would give to a plaintiff in this case under the facts of this case that would put a zero in for punitive damages and tell those members of the Board of Directors, tell Mr. Sarchett, tell Mr. Shernoff, that this is not the case to punish Blue Shield.

"Thank you very much."

The jury *did* decide to punish Blue Shield. John Sarchett was awarded $100,000: $20,000 for mental distress and $80,000 in punitive damages. Although the award was not as large as I had hoped for, a significant issue was resolved. Now maybe Blue Shield would be forced to change its ways.

I thought that Blue Shield might decide to pay the judgment. After all, this was the second time the company had tried the same issue and lost. Since the jury did not know of the earlier arbitration award, the verdicts were independent of one another. However, Blue Shield decided to appeal. For the appeal, we brought into the case Leonard Sacks, a brilliant legal writer and scholar, who assists us in all our appeals. The appeal took almost 3 years. It seemed like an eternity. Finally, on January 2, 1987, the California Supreme Court ruled that coverage would be afforded to a policyholder, such as Sarchett, unless the insurance company could prove that the treating physician's judgment was plainly unreasonable or contrary to good medical practice. In short, an insurance company will not be able to overrule judgments of treating doctors on questions of medical necessity, unless it has evidence demonstrating that the doctor is doing something contrary to good medical practice. After a long legal struggle, the Sarchett case produced valuable law in situations where insurance companies overrule judgments of treating physicians.

However, in John's case, the judge ruled Blue Shield was guilty of bad faith and the California Supreme Court held that this should have been for the jury to decide. So they ordered another trial. For John this meant going back to trial for the third time on his original $1,200 hospital bill. The case was now almost ten years old. Both John and I were getting tired of it. It was like going to see a movie for the third time. We decided an out-of-court settlement would be appropriate since the law now had been established. So, John ended up taking a favorable out-of-court settlement that required Blue Shield to pay over 30 times the amount of the original hospital bill.

\* \* \*

"It's a shame. We are victims because we allow ourselves to be victims."

Barbara Visconti, dying of heart disease at the age of fifty-three, spoke those words to me near the end of her life. She died before her victory against Blue Cross of California, but she fought a courageous battle up to the end.

Thinking she was well protected by her Blue Cross major medical policy, Barbara felt secure when she was hospitalized in December 1979. Her insurance policy was the one bit of comfort she had after learning that she was suffering from severe cardiomyopathy, a disease that would swell her heart muscles and eventually kill her. There was no cure.

She spent several weeks in the hospital in San Diego, California, and was finally released with the recommendation that she arrange for skilled nursing care at home. The side effects and the toxicity of the drugs she took required constant monitoring. She was coming home to die, and the skilled nursing care she had arranged would make it possible for her to die in as dignified a manner as possible. She assumed that the $1,400 weekly cost for round-the-clock care would be paid by her Blue Cross major-medical health plan. Her son and daughter-in-law Steve and Naomi Lesberg, checked with Barbara's Blue Cross agent who assured them the policy would cover the home nursing care. All that would be required, said the agent, was a letter from her doctor explaining that the skilled care was essential to Barbara's health and well-being.

Her doctor wrote the required letter, and Barbara submitted the nursing-care bills to Blue Cross for payment. Indeed, five months of bills were submitted to the health-plan office before Blue Cross wrote Barbara and told her that the company would not pay the bills, any of them. In the interim, she had taken money from her savings account to pay the nurses.

After the denial, the Lesbergs panicked. They contacted someone in the San Diego Blue Cross office who told them to get a more definitive letter from Barbara's doctor. Her cardiologist, Marshall Franklin, wrote Blue Cross affirming that "Barbara cannot exist outside a hospital atmosphere without skilled nursing help at home."

Blue Cross chose to disbelieve Dr. Franklin's clearly stated and well-founded opinion and instead decided that the care Barbara received at home was "custodial" care rather than skilled care. Barbara's policy did not cover "custodial" nursing. The company then concluded her expenses were not eligible for Blue Cross payments. The fine-line distinction the Blues make between custodial, for which they do not pay, and skilled care, for which they are required to pay, was familiar to me. I had handled other cases which involved the same "distinction." However, none of the cases seemed as blatant as this one.

A custodial nurse is licensed to bathe and feed patients and, in general, to keep them comfortable. Skilled care nurses are licensed to do all of the custodial functions plus give injections, administer medicines, help evaluate symptoms. A skilled nurse assists in treating the patient. There was no clear definition of skilled or custodial care in Barbara's insurance policy, and we believed that Blue Cross was acting in its own interests by refusing to pay for Barbara's care.

By July 1980, Barbara had run out of savings. She owed over $20,000 to her nurses, who declared they could no longer work without being paid. The Lesbergs came to the rescue by converting their garage into a makeshift hospital. Naomi Lesberg nursed her mother-in-law in the best way she knew how. Despite Barbara's weak and declining health, she knew that Blue Cross was denying money that was rightfully hers. She was very angry and she told her daughter-in-law that she wanted to fight.

The Lesbergs had heard of our cases against insurance companies and they contacted my partner, Harvey Levine, who runs our San Diego office. Harvey was a good choice for them. He is a brilliant lawyer and former law professor. He and I began our friendship some years before when he sought my advice on a case while he was teaching at the University of San Diego Law School. Eventually, I persuaded him to leave the lofty world of academia for the trenches of trial work. He has quickly become one of the most successful trial lawyers in California and an ardent advocate of the oppressed.

Harvey filed the lawsuit soon after Barbara and her family told us their sad story. The complaint read like an indictment.

"Blue Cross refused to pay the nursing bills after advising Barbara they would be covered.

"Blue Cross refused to speak to Barbara about her claim.

"Blue Cross refused to meet with Barbara

personally for the purpose of determining the severity of her condition.

"Blue Cross consciously disregarded the opinion of Barbara's treating doctors that skilled nursing care was essential to her health and comfort.

"Blue Cross refused to discuss Barbara's condition with her doctors.

"Blue Cross failed to obtain Barbara's medical and hospital records.

"Blue Cross refused to discuss the nature of the skilled nursing care with the skilled nurses who worked at Barbara's home for six months.

"Blue Cross had unqualified claims people make medical decisions about Barbara's need for skilled care.

"Blue Cross consciously disregarded Barbara's medical needs."

Harvey had thrown in everything but the kitchen sink because he wanted Blue Cross's attention. The complaint also included information gleaned from letters back and forth between the family and Blue Cross. Harvey pointed out that eventually the family had engaged in nothing short of begging for reimbursement.

The lawsuit was filed but before the case came to court, Barbara Visconti died with debts and without the dignity she had sought. Harvey and I were very upset. We vowed to continue her fight. We were infuriated by the realization that for the last months of her life she had lived in a converted garage without the skilled nursing care she required. In her conversation with us, Mrs. Visconti had said time and again that the system was wrong, that it needed bucking, and that she wanted to fight the Blues to victory.

The case came up for trial about a year after Barbara's death. Under California law, it is not possible to claim damages for mental distress for persons already deceased, but the claims for medical bills and punitive damages remained valid. In fact, the case would now be concerned primarily with punitive damages. Barbara had wanted to set an example. We knew what she had suffered, and we were determined to punish Blue Cross in a big way.

We were aware that Blue Cross wasn't feeling very good about the case because shortly before the trial date the company paid the nursing care bills; a little late for Barbara, but it was at least some acknowledgment on the company's part that she had been right.

The day before the trial was due to start, Judge F. B. Lopardo, San Diego Superior Court, called the two sides in for a settlement conference. He heard both sides of the story, and he then told Blue Cross lawyers they would be in for big trouble from a jury. The company's three lawyers and a Blue Cross claims examiner seemed to take the judge's admonitions to heart, and after a relatively short time, they came to the conclusion the ball was in our court.

Harvey and I decided we would accept no offer less than $400,000. The first Blue Cross offer was $100,000. We rejected it quickly. We were perfectly willing to go all the way and to have a jury decide the amount. Within a couple of hours, Blue Cross agreed to $400,000. The money went into Barbara's estate.

Neither Harvey nor I will forget Barbara's courage and her tenacity. She was willing to buck the Blues from her deathbed in a converted garage. She was right: We all become victims when we allow ourselves to be victimized.

# Chapter 4

# Justin's Car

Southern California is smoggy. Even healthy people have trouble breathing when the air gets really bad. It is worse for a handicapped boy like Justin Ingram. Joe and Mary Ingram dedicated their lives to Justin, their only child. Justin was suffering from severe muscular dystrophy, and Justin's doctor told Joe and Mary that the smog was a decided irritant to the boy's health. Joe and Mary decided to leave their Pomona, California home for the high desert city of Winchester, where the air was cleaner and would be healthier for Justin.

The Ingrams found their new settlement pleasant. Joe was a truck driver, and he could drive just as easily from Winchester as from Pomona. Mary enjoyed the desert community. Their only problem was the 60 miles to the Kaiser Hospital in Fontana, where Justin underwent medical treatment. In addition to Justin's regular treatment at Kaiser, Justin was due for a special surgical procedure and recovery follow-up that required a 100-mile trip to Children's Hospital in San Diego.

The family owned an old Plymouth that had traveled 200,000 miles. It was their only car and not dependable. Joe decided to invest all his money on a down payment on a new 1975 Oldsmobile station wagon. The new wagon, called "Justin's car," was delivered three days before Justin was due for his operation in San Diego.

Justin had the operation, and his postoperative plaster cast stretched from his waist to his toes. The station wagon enabled the Ingrams to bring Justin and his wheelchair home after the operation.

Joe Ingram was a great believer in insurance and had insurance on nearly everything. When he bought the station wagon, he bought a credit disability policy with Commercial Bankers Life Insurance Company. This kind of insurance promises to make installment payments if a time-payment buyer becomes disabled. The coverage made Joe feel secure. He thought that if anything happened to him, the insurance company would take over the payments, and Justin would still have the use of the new station wagon.

Soon after he bought the car, Joe injured his back. He had a rigorous job driving semis for General Cable Corporation, and, in addition, he had to load and unload huge reels of cables. At times he had to use a twenty-pound sledgehammer to break a reel loose from its harness. The job was heavy-duty labor, difficult enough for a person with a good back, but impossible for someone with a bad one.

When Joe began treatments for his back injury, he filed a claim with Commercial Bankers. Immediately the insurance company became Joe's adversary. Disputes took place over every aspect of his disability, including a proposed doctor's examination. Commercial Bankers made a couple of installment payments on the station wagon, but refused to continue unless Joe agreed to an independent medical exam. Joe had no quarrel with this request, but, as he wrote Commercial Bankers in June 1976:

"Dear Sir:

I will be glad to have a doctor of your choice to examine me any time you want. There are several orthopedic doctors in Hemet, which is only five miles from my home. Pick one of them out, and I will be glad to go.

In regard to my claim, I was examined by Dr. Mueller on April 26, 1976, who documented my last report. I was examined on June 3rd by Dr. Roback, 6221 Wilshire Boulevard, Los Angeles. I feel this is more than sufficient proof of my disability.

Your company only has my account for my benefits paid through April 30, 1976. I see no reason why you shouldn't bring it up to date. I bought this insurance in good faith and paid over $300 for it. On numerous occasions I have called your Sherman Oaks office, and they were uncooperative and sarcastic. They treated Mr. Vaness the same way. He is with Security Pacific National Bank in Hemet, California. The bank keeps calling me. They have even come out to my house. They have threatened to repossess my car. This is all due to your company not paying my benefits in a reasonable amount of time. This is causing a lot of worry and emotional stress on me and my wife. Your kind attention is appreciated.

Yours truly,

Joe Ingram."

Although Commercial Bankers originally wanted Joe to go to a doctor two hours away in Los Angeles, they agreed eventually with Joe's request for a local doctor. Joe went to his appointment with Dr. Joseph Klein in nearby Hemet. Joe thought the examination would show Commercial Bankers his claim was legitimate. Dr. Klein even agreed to treat Joe regularly for his bad back. Commercial Bankers had a different point of view.

Meanwhile, Security Pacific was getting increasingly insistent about their car payments. The bank sent a representative out to Joe's house. Joe was not home at the time, and Mary was given a good scare. Joe called the bank, and the officials assured him that no action would be taken to repossess the car before Joe was informed. The conversation reassured Joe. He felt sure that once Commercial Bankers saw Dr. Klein's report, the car payments would resume.

Suddenly, in August 1976, an event took place that sent Joe flying into my office. We were considering the filing of a lawsuit at once. What happened is best explained three years later on May 10, 1979, when I had Joe tell his story from the witness stand.

Joe explained how he had thought his problem with Commercial Bankers was about to be resolved, how things seemed to be straightening out. Then, one morning, while on errands and one day after he had the conversation with the bank, he got the surprise of his life. This was the way Joe described it to the jury:

Ingram:  "I was in the post office getting my mail. As I was walking out the door, a young male was in my car.

"He just started it up, and I yelled at him to get out of my car. And he saw me, and he gunned the car, jumped about an 18-inch curb. I yelled at him again to stop, that he was in my car; and I started to chase after him.

"From that point he jumped the curb, to the stop sign, was maybe 50 or 60 feet.

"People came running out of the little grocery store there. This guy run the stop sign onto the highway with my automobile and it scared me quite a bit.

"I went in the store, was going to call the highway patrol, the sheriff or any law enforcement agency that I could get ahold of. I was shaking too bad to dial the phone number. So Pat Parkhurst, the gentleman who owns the store, he dialed the sheriff and the highway patrol, and the highway patrol sheriff's cars came out.

"The highway patrol asked me to call—
first they asked me if my car had been
repossessed, and I said no, it hasn't been
repossessed. I said it was stolen. And
they asked me to call the bank who had it
financed to make double sure before
they picked the guy up that took the car.

"And I called the bank, and at that time
they informed me that the car had been
repossessed. The order had been put out
the day before."

Shernoff: "Now, at the time your car was taken
from you, if you knew that it was going to
be repossessed, would you have
attempted to make other arrangements
to make the payment, yourself?"

A. "Yes. I would have borrowed money
from my younger brother who lives in
Santa Monica."

Q. "That new Oldsmobile was very
important to you, wasn't it?"

A. "Extremely important."

Q. "Would you say that was your most
important possession?"

A. "Yes, sir, it was."

Q. "Did you expect that, if the insurance
company was going to stop making
payments to the bank, that they would
have notified you before they told the
bank that they weren't going to make
any more payments?"

A. "Yes, sir. I suspected they would give me

that courtesy. I couldn't believe—I had no doubt that the insurance company was going to make the payments, because of all the documented doctor's proof that I had."

Q. "Now, when the repossession occurred, were you embarrassed and humiliated?"

A. "Yes, sir. I didn't suspect the car was going to be repossessed. When it was stolen from me at the post office, I knew that it was stolen, and that's the only thing I had in my mind.

"There were a few people there then, especially after—I think there were three or four CHP [California Highway Patrol] and sheriff's cars at the scene. People gathered there in the little market and were all standing around when the CHP officers wanted me to call the bank to verify whether or not the car had, in fact, been repossessed, which I did. And everyone in the store heard that conversation, and in the back of their minds was, 'There is another bum, doesn't pay his bills.'

"They didn't know what the circumstances were, why the car was repossessed, because the payments were not made on it. And that humiliated me very much, it embarrassed me."

Q. "Other than the conversation in the store, do you know if the fact that your car got repossessed got around the community in Winchester?"

A. "Yes, sir. Before the car was taken from the post office, the same people who took the car were on my neighbor's property at about four or 4:30 A.M. that morning. Her husband was gone, and she was there with four or five children, and she had gotten on her CB radio, and it was all over the CB radios in that area that the car had been stolen. And then, after that, they found out it had been repossessed."

Right after the repossession, as soon as he regained his composure, Joe called Commercial Bankers to find out what was going on. I asked him to tell the jury what the insurance company said.

Ingram: "I tried to call the president and vice-president of Commercial Bankers Insurance Company person-to-person on Friday, the same day the car was taken. Whoever it was answering the phone, wanted to know what it was in regard to. I gave the operator just a small amount of what it was about, and she put me on hold; and then she came back and said that they would contact me.

"So, the following Monday I received a letter from Commercial Bankers Insurance Company, dated August the 13th, it said that they were not going to pay my claim, and that Dr. Klein said there wasn't anything wrong with me."

I had first learned this story from a letter Joe wrote asking for my help. It was a three-page handwritten document. The letter ended with these words:

"I've never hated anyone or anything, nor have I

ever been so humiliated, or embarrassed, as I was when they put me through an actual robbery, when they stole my car. I now know what it is to hate. I want revenge on Commercial Bankers in the greatest way. My limited vocabularly cannot describe the mental, physical, or the anguish this has caused me and my family or the great burden this has put on myself, knowing my son's car has wrongfully been taken from him. I am unable to work to provide him with what he needs. I have worked very hard to provide for my family, I worked very hard to acquire my car and faithfully paid for insurance for car payments so that my family would have certain provisions in case of an emergency. Now, even this has been stripped from my family's well-being.

When I first read this letter, I thought Commercial Bankers had made a mistake. I asked Joe to write Commercial Bankers a letter because, under California law, a person has a little time to recover repossessed property, and I thought if Joe explained what had happened, Commercial Bankers might reevaluate their position. Joe wrote the letter but got no response.

The jury sat quiet and breathless as Joe read the letter aloud, about how he'd been examined by at least five doctors, and all agreed Joe was disabled and no longer fit for his strenuous work. One doctor advised him not to stand or sit in any one position for more than thirty minutes and, therefore, he could no longer drive a truck. The letter described in technical detail what the doctors told Joe was happening to his spine and the treatments he required. At one point in the letter Joe's voice began to quiver:

Ingram: "I am trying to get my back repaired so I
    · can return to work. The reason why I
    bought a new station wagon last year was

because my son has a serious disease. My wife has to take him to Kaiser Hospital in Fontana, some 60 miles away, and the station wagon would be more comfortable for him, as my old Plymouth just wasn't reliable enough for my wife and son to make frequent trips to the hospital."

When Joe finished reading he broke down and sobbed. I asked the judge if I could finish reading Joe's letter. The judge said that would be a good idea. I turned to the jury and continued.

Shernoff: "Just recently we found out we are going to have to start taking Justin to Children's Hospital in San Diego, some 70 miles each way; and now, because you are refusing to live up to the terms of the insurance written by your company, I will have to attempt to get him there in a 1965 Plymouth with over 200,000 miles on it.

"Our 1975 station wagon was repossessed about 8:30 A.M. August 13th, 1976. No one notified me of this until August 19th, 1976. They didn't ask me for it, or knock on my door.

"They put me through an actual robbery. They stole it from me while I was in the U.S. Post Office in Winchester, and I yelled at them to stop, but they didn't. I called the police. The police arrived and asked me to call the bank to see if it was repossessed. I made this call inside the Winchester market. The bank told me they repossessed my car. This whole episode was witnessed by other people, and I have never been so humiliated or embarrassed.

"Would you please reconsider my claim? I'm asking for an eight-year-old boy who is seriously ill and is in dire need of a reliable automobile. Your kind and prompt attention concerning this matter will be greatly appreciated. Would you please send me a copy of Dr. Klein's report, dated July 29th, 1976?

"The bank notified me I only have until the 23rd of this month to resolve this matter. Would you please send me your immediate reply? Yours very truly, Joe Ingram."

I finished reading the letter to the jury, and then I asked Joe:

Shernoff: "Mr. Ingram, did anybody from the insurance company telephone you in response to this letter?"

Ingram: "No, sir, they didn't."

Q. "You did receive a letter from Commercial Bankers after you wrote this, did you not?"

A. "No, sir, I didn't."

Q. "None, whatsoever?"

A. "None."

Joe and his wife then testified that they began using the Plymouth to transport Justin. Mary said that the fumes from the Plymouth made Justin sick. One time the muffler actually caught fire and burned a hole through the floor.

Their testimony showed that these were bad times for the family. Desperately in need of money to pay debts and live, Joe eventually filed bankruptcy and sold his house.

The next witness was Dr. Joseph Klein. I thought that Dr. Klein, the independent medical examiner for Commercial Bankers, would be the key to Justin's case. I had to prove that Commercial Bankers misinterpreted Dr. Klein's report deliberately in order to justify its refusal to pay Joe's car payments. I wanted to show that Dr. Klein's medical report was, through no fault of his own, incomplete.

Dr. Klein had been asked to conduct his examination in a vacuum. He received no medical history and no job description. He thought he was to determine whether Joe could perform *any* kind of work *at all*. Dr. Klein's report to Commercial Bankers was therefore ambiguous. The doctor did find that Joe had serious back problems and recommended that he wear a special support corset, have physical therapy, and be placed in cervical and pelvic traction.

As Dr. Klein was testifying, I explained Joe's job to him. I asked the doctor what he thought about Joe's loading and unloading huge reels of cable in his disabled condition.

> Klein: "I think, under the circumstances, I don't believe I would recommend that he do that sort of activity. I think maybe he could, you know, swing a sledgehammer a couple of times and knock some nails out; but I think, under the circumstances, that it would not be a good idea."

> Shernoff: "And you wouldn't recommend it, would you?"

> A. "I would not recommend him doing something that would aggravate his condition, no."

Q. "How about doing this type of activity for, let's say, an hour straight?"

A. "No, I would not recommend that."

Q. "Would you, medically speaking, say Mr. Ingram was disabled from doing that sort of work?"

A. "Yes."

This testimony was a big blow to Commercial Bankers' case. The bottom-line issue in the case was whether Joe's disability prevented him from doing his job. The only thing Commercial Bankers had to justify their refusal to pay Joe's disability claim was Dr. Klein's report and here he was in court, blowing them out of the water.

The lawyer for Commercial Bankers was Tim Sargent, a very able man from Los Angeles. He tried hard to shake Dr. Klein's testimony, but to no avail. The jury must have wondered how Commercial Bankers could have put the Ingrams through so much torture on the basis of Dr. Klein's report when the jury had just heard Dr. Klein say that Joe was disabled and could not do his job. Surely if Dr. Klein had received proper information in the first place, and had been asked the proper questions by the insurance company, his report would have been the same as his testimony in court.

After a few other witnesses were called, the closing arguments began. I don't believe I have ever been as angry in court as I was when I began this argument. I was suffering right along with Joe, Mary, and Justin. My state of mind was obvious.

"I submit to you, ladies and gentlemen, if this is good faith and fair dealing. Is this guarding Joe's rights with trust and fidelity? Is this the way you'd like your rights guarded with trust and fidelity?

"As soon as Commercial Bankers received Dr. Klein's

report, they sent a letter to Mr. Ingram telling him that Dr. Klein said he could work as a truck driver. Dr. Klein didn't [say] that, at all. As a matter of fact, if Commercial Bankers had invested a dollar for a phone call, Dr. Klein would have told them exactly what he told you folks. There would have been no problem. The minute they get that report, they say, 'Okay, that's it. No more payments.' They don't check with the bank. They don't check with Mr. Ingram. Boom. That's it. Cast off. Off you go. You're on your own.

"The repossession at the post office is incredible. Until I got this case, I didn't even know things like that could still happen. You go to the post office and someone takes your car away, and your personal possessions that are in it.... But it goes from bad to worse. Mr. Ingram writes them a letter and explains. A three-page letter. Even after the repossession, he is giving them another chance.

"He said, 'I have been embarrassed. I have been humiliated. I'm asking for an eight-year-old boy who is seriously ill and in dire need of a reliable automobile....[I am] very hard-pressed financially ...[I] don't have the funds to repair my old Plymouth...[we] require a reliable automobile... your kind and prompt attention...'

"Frankly, I think Mr. Ingram is displaying a lot of good character. If my car was repossessed or if it was my boy....I would never write a letter asking for kind and prompt attention. My letter would have some words in there that would make your hair curl."

I became so wound up that I made a remark that was probably out of bounds:

Shernoff: "Is this guarding his rights? They ought to be embarrassed. If I had to use my law degree to come in and defend garbage like this, I'd throw it away."

Sargent: "Your Honor, I object to that. I resent it as a personal attack on counsel, a violation of canons of ethics, and improper argument."

Shernoff: "I am sorry for getting carried away. I apologize to counsel."

Sargent: "Thank you, Mr. Shernoff."

After I finished, Tim Sargent tried to calm the atmosphere in the courtroom. He did a good job. He reviewed practically every point of the testimony and attempted to identify inconsistencies. He tried to show that Joe may have been responsible for part of the problem by not cooperating with Commercial Bankers. He concluded by stating:

"I don't think that the conduct of Commercial Bankers is any more unreasonable than the conduct of Mr. Ingram. I think that is what you will find. That is why you will find a defense verdict. I put Commercial Bankers into your hands."

The jury took Commercial Bankers in its hands and squeezed. It took one day to reach the verdict. On May 21, 1979, the jurors awarded Joe $128,000 for mental and emotional distress and $872,001 in punitive damages. The total was $1,000,001. Later on, I asked the jury foreman why they decided for the odd figure of $1 over $1 million. The jury, he said, wanted this unusual amount so Commercial Bankers would remember it. I was elated and the Ingrams felt vindicated. I thought that justice had been done.

The Ingrams were very grateful to the Muscular Dystrophy Association for all its help with Justin, and Joe told me he wanted to donate half of the punitive damage award to the Muscular Dystrophy Association. I thought this was terrific, and I immediately contacted MDA in New York to tell them of Joe's charity. They were pleased and within a day or two, I was contacted by their lawyer.

On July 3, 1979, Joe signed an agreement donating, "one-half of his net recovery of punitive damages to do the research and development necessary to find a cure or otherwise alleviate the effects of the duchenne-type muscular dystrophy." MDA agreed to earmark the money for specific research projects. Ninety percent (90%) of all funds received would be spent for specific research projects and none of the funds would be spent for administrative costs. The donation was to be known as the "Justin Ingram" trust fund.

We were well satisfied until a bomb dropped on us. Commercial Bankers made the usual motion for a new trial. I did not think the motion would be granted because I felt the evidence was strong and that Commercial Bankers deserved severe punishment. The judge felt otherwise. He granted Commercial Bankers a new trial unless we agreed to a reduction of the compensatory damages in the amount of $35,000 and agreed to eliminate punitive damages altogether. I could not believe it. Riverside County Superior Court Judge J. David Hennigan was a man I respected and admired. I had known him when he was a lawyer, and I knew he had a people-oriented practice. That made it even harder to understand when he came out against us.

The law which permits a judge to grant a new trial or reduce verdicts is complicated. Although there are different viewpoints, generally a trial judge may reduce a jury's verdict if he feels—after reweighing all the evidence —that the facts do not support the verdict. Most people do not know about this law. Indeed, it makes little sense to have a full-blown jury trial, to let a jury set an amount, and then have the judge impose his own idea of what the appropriate amount should be. Understandably, a judge should grant a new trial when a prejudicial legal error occurs or where one side does not receive a fair trial. In the case of Justin's car, the judge did not find a legal error. He acknowledged the trial was fair; he simply thought that the evidence did not support the verdict. I disagreed, but there was nothing I could do except file an appeal with the District Court of Appeal. Then I went into a depression that lasted weeks.

Appeals take a long time in California, and two or three years is commonplace. This delay was placing a great financial burden on the Ingrams because they were bankrupt and matters were getting worse. After our appeal had been on file for about a year, Joe came to me in desperation. He wanted me to take a stab at settling. I was sure the insurance company would not pay anything near what the verdict had been. After all, Commercial Bankers now had the upper hand. I approached Tim Sargent on the subject, and he was very understanding. After some negotiations he came through with a $100,000 settlement offer. Joe's only choice was to accept it. Since the jury's original award was $128,000 in compensatory damages, the settlement amounted to $28,000 less compensation and zero for punitive damages. Still, $100,000 was a lot of money for Joe and allowed the family to start a new life and get on their feet again.

Because Joe received no money for punitive damages, he could not make Justin's donation to the Muscular Dystrophy Association. On October 22, 1980, I wrote the Association and explained:

> "Under these circumstances, we have advised Mr. Ingram that he is not obligated to the Muscular Dystrophy Association under the terms of the agreement. However, knowing Mr. Ingram, he may very well voluntarily decide to contribute. We have told him that that is strictly up to him.

"We feel this result was unfortunate....Money that would have been available for an extremely worthy cause has become unavailable because of the trial judge's decision to nullify the jury's verdict.

"Indeed, this is a graphic example of a citizen who, economically, could not afford to appeal. The trial judge had put him in an untenable position because of the new trial order.

"What even distresses me more, is that in this particular case, we had a trial judge whom I respect as being one of the best on the bench. He is extremely intelligent, and is philosophically in favor of the jury system. If this can happen with such a sensitive judge then it is time to start figuring out ways to make a jury trial mean something more than just a nice-sounding phrase."

Since *Ingram* v. *Commercial Bankers*, I have worked hard to change the law that allows a judge to reduce a jury's verdict. I have deep respect for our jury system. I have tried to rationalize the judge's decision by blaming the system that would allow this to occur. I figured that Judge Hennigan must have had a good reason for his decision. But since I could not talk to him about it, to this day I do not know the reason for his ruling. The next year I was elected president of the California Trial Lawyers Association (CTLA). I devoted a substantial amount of time attempting to introduce legislation that would cure this defect in the law.

I spent most of 1981 at the state capitol in Sacramento. I discovered quickly that legislation lobbying is not an easy task. The first thing I realized was that while the insurance lobby is very strong, there is no organized lobby for the policyholder except the various trial lawyer organizations. I hoped to change the law that allowed the unjust result in the *Ingram* case. I also wanted to get a law passed that would make insurance companies pay interest to an injured victim from the day a lawsuit is filed, rather than from the date of a court judgment, which usually is years later.

The lobbyist for the California Trial Lawyers Association was Jim Frayne. He had been in the capitol for years and really knew the ropes. He took me aside and told me how things worked in Sacramento. He said, "Bill, here everything goes by the golden rule—the people that have the gold make the rules."

The insurance industry vigorously opposes any change in the law that allows a judge to reduce jury verdicts. That law still remains, but we will keep trying to change it. However, with a great effort by many trial lawyers, we were able to convince the legislature to pass a prejudgment-interest law. The law makes it possible, in some cases, to collect interest on damages from the day a lawsuit is filed.

The *Ingram* case was an enlightening experience. It convinced me of the value of our civil jury system and what it means to the average citizen. The jury is truly the cornerstone of our system of justice. We, as a society, should guard constantly against attempts to weaken it for the sake of efficiency or advantage by any one group. The weaker our jury system becomes, the less valuable our individual rights become.

# Chapter 5

# Do You Have to Be a Prisoner in Your House to Collect?

In America insurance policies may as well be written in hieroglyphics. They are nearly impossible to decipher, one incomprehensible clause after another. Worse, the important points for the consumer are usually hidden in a sea of fine print.

One of my favorite fine print gems is a clause, known in insurance jargon, as the "house confinement" clause. This clause, common to disability-insurance policies, prevents a disabled person from receiving benefits unless he leads a prisonlike existence in his own house.

Here is how a typical house-confinement clause reads:

> If sickness confines the insured within doors for one day or more and requires regular treatment by a licensed physician, the company will pay benefits periodically at the rate of the regular monthly benefits so long as such confinement continues.

A reasonable person might interpret this to mean that benefits will continue as long as the person is sick enough to have to spend most of his time at home. The insurance industry doesn't see it this way. Carriers use this clause against their policyholders in outrageous ways, and for this reason, the clause is unconscionable and should be outlawed.

I have known people who were totally disabled with heart disease, back problems and cancer, completely unable to work, yet, because they were able to leave their houses on small errands or do a little socializing, their insurance benefits have been refused.

These days the whole world knows that exercise of some sort is often prescribed for most illnesses. Patients with everything from heart problems to psychiatric difficulties are encouraged to walk, bicycle, or swim to keep their bodies functioning. Insurance companies have yet to figure out that house-confinement clauses shouldn't mean that policyholders must be shackled to their beds.

Insurance companies require that disability policyholders have a medical form filled out by their doctors. The form usually includes a question about whether or not the patient is house-confined. If the doctor checks "no" because he realizes his patient must get out, even if just to see the doctor, the insurance company may use his answer to deny benefits. Generally, there is no definition in the policy for "house confinement."

Fortunately, courts have given liberal interpretations to house-confinement clauses. In Arkansas a court held that a man had not violated the house-confinement clause by taking talks and visiting friends at work. The court even allowed the man to work on occasional Saturdays as a salesman. In Minnesota a mentally disabled person was within his house-confinement clause even though he left home for recreation, shopping, and doing menial tasks off and on. A Tennessee court allowed a house-confined insured to take trips away from home to relieve tension. In Oklahoma a court declined to enforced a house-confinement clause that required the insured to remain, in all circumstances, under his roof. A Louisiana court decided a heart attack victim was entitled to his benefits even though his wife took him on a monthly 35-mile drive to visit their daughter; the man also took a daily walk to his mailbox.

The very first bad faith case to come out of California, *Wetherbee* v. *United Insurance Company,* involved a house-confinement clause. Wetherbee's insurance carrier denied benefits because she was not "house-confined." She was denied benefits because she had the audacity to attend church several times and to attend a couple of club meetings. She was awarded $200,000 in punitive damages by a California jury.

Most of these cases are more than twenty years old. One would think by now that the insurance industry would get the message that juries frown upon the use of house-confinement clauses to deny disabled people their benefits. The industry, however, is as undaunted as it is arrogant.

I particularly remember a case I handled for Morris Bronstein. Morris was fifty-five and ran a small retail liquor shop with his wife. His business involved the day-to-day routine of stocking, selling, and administering a small package-goods store. One day Morris felt some chest pains. He went to his doctor. The diagnosis was coronary heart disease. A special diet, an exercise program, and nitrogylcerin pills were prescribed. Nothing helped, and his condition deteriorated. Even though his medication was increased, Morris continued to suffer chest pains and terrible fatigue. His doctor declared him totally disabled and recommended that he give up the liquor business or risk death. Morris heeded the doctor's advice and quit working.

Morris and his wife then moved to Palm Springs. They hoped the desert climate would improve his health. Morris subsequently put in a claim for disability benefits on his two policies with Benefit Trust Life Insurance Company. Morris expected to collect $600 disability benefits per month. It was well after he was disabled that Morris discovered the house-confinement clause in one of his policies. Benefit Trust paid benefits for one year, then notified Morris that his regular checks would stop because "the medical information we have received shows that your illness has not confined you to your house."

This was true. Morris was not chained to his house. After he moved to Palm Springs, he continued his prescribed regimen of walking and taking his pills when chest pains came on. The rest of the time, he read, watched television, played gin rummy with his wife, and sat around. His life was regulated and careful. There was little socializing. Once, when he wanted to take a little trip, he got his doctor's okay for a house-trailer excursion.

We filed a bad faith suit on behalf of Morris. During the trial, the insurance-company claims manager who had made the decision to terminate Morris's benefits testified that it was his belief that under a house-confinement clause, no social activities could take place. I decided to test just how far his beliefs went:

Shernoff:  "Now just so I understand you correctly, you said visits to the doctor would be permissible?"

A.  "Yes."

Q.  "And perhaps a therapuetic walk would be permissible?"

A.  "Yes."

Q.  "Anything else?"

A.  "No."

Q.  "Now, sir, I believe you said social activities would not be permissible."

A.  "That's correct."

Q.  "Let's take for example some totally disabled person who wants to go to a ball game, let's say the World Series. If he did that, would that cut off his benefits?"

A. "You mean as a one-time deal or on a constant basis?"

Q. "Let's make it one-time first; I'll make him a fan after a while."

A. "On a one-time basis, I would think that might sort of be open for discussion."

Q. "Well, the reason I asked is because you said social activities are not permissible and I just took a baseball game as being a social activity. Are you saying that there might be social activities that would be permitted?"

A. "Okay, I would say no, the baseball game would not be permitted."

Q. "Could this actually serve to terminate his benefits?"

A. "Yes."

Q. "Would that be true, sir, even for—let's say a quadraplegic who went in a wheelchair?"

A. "Yes."

When the trial ended, the jury awarded Morris $24,800 for disability benefits up to the time of trial; $72,000 in future disability benefits; $2,000 in emotional-distress payments; and $150,000 in punitive damages.

The *Bronstein* case, one of my first bad faith trials, opened the door for significant house-confinement-clause victories. It also led to my association with Will Denton, a lawyer from Biloxi, Mississippi, whose southern accent alone could charm a victory out of a jury. I met Denton at an American Trial Lawyers convention in New Orleans. He was representing several disability clients whose benefits had been terminated because of house-confinement clauses. We decided to join forces. I thought it would be challenging to work in the Deep South, and I thought maybe I could bring California's brand of justice to the Mississippi insurance industry.

Trial work in Mississippi is not like trial work in California, and the experience was interesting. Despite my army experience, I was not used to the southern courtroom style. I was surprised when I saw the first witness sworn in on a Bible. I had seen that before only on television.

The first case we worked on was for a self-employed laborer named Wilfred Fayard who injured his back while he was carrying a bathtub. He lost disability benefits when his insurance company decided he wasn't obeying the house-confinement rules. Like Morris Bronstein in California, Fayard managed to walk a few hundred yards every day for exercise prescribed by his doctor.

During the trial, a former claims adjuster testified that some of the carrier's field representatives were under a quota to close half of their policyholders' claims. This technique applied across the board regardless of the validity of the claim. The jury found bad faith and awarded Fayard $175,000. We eventually collected $250,000 when the insurance company conceded that Fayard would be owed future benefits of another $75,000.

In another case, we represented Wilfred Shaw, who sued his insurance company for bad faith after a company agent coerced him into admitting he was not literally house-confined. He signed away his policy for a nominal amount. This is how attorney Will Denton explains the case:

> "The mode of operation at that time was to have field adjusters identify potential lifetime cases. There is a sinister meaning to that. Remember now, these disability policies are touted as being lifetime policies, noncancellable, guaranteed, etc., etc. The obligation of the insurance company is to act on behalf of the insured. Instead, this company did the

opposite. They had an internal system set up to recognize potential lifetime cases and then to terminate them.

"In Mr. Shaw's case, a field representative came out on a Sunday afternoon. You have to understand, the Shaws are country people, close, nice, quiet country people and you can imagine how they might react to such a visit. Mr. Shaw was on medical disability and classified as house-confined. He was in bed at the time of the adjuster's visit. The agent told Mr. Shaw he had been seen riding around in his car with his wife who, it turned out, had been driving Mr. Shaw to the doctor. The field representative said Mr. Shaw had also been seen working in his yard. The adjuster told him his policy said he had to be house-confined. 'We know you're an honest man,' he told Mr. Shaw, 'and that you wouldn't want to cheat the company. I'll tell you what we're going to do. We're going to pay you $700, a couple months' benefits, and you'll sign a release for us.'

"Well, the representative wrote out a release right then, no witnesses, not even Mrs. Shaw, and Mr. Shaw signed it. He signed the release which said he admitted he was no longer house-confined and he signed away what could have been $30,000 worth of benefits. I viewed this set of facts as being outrageous. Bill Shernoff and I eventually settled the case for $190,000."

These "house-confinement" cases prove that juries will get angry at insurance companies for shortchanging their policyholders no matter where the courtroom is. There are not enough lawyers to handle these cases. Bad faith law is so new that most law schools do not teach bad faith courses. I spend a great deal of time lecturing to trial lawyer associations about the law, and I hope this will inspire young lawyers to pursue bad faith cases in their home states. I believe that we need an army of trial lawyers to protect the public from insurance company abuse.

# Chapter 6

# A Piece of the Rock

Uncovering elaborate insurance schemes often requires great effort. Yet, in some cases, the testimony of insurance agents is so deplorable that little digging is necessary. That was the case with Raymond Pistorius, a forty-two year old truck driver who decided to battle Prudential, the largest insurance company in America.

For almost twenty years Ray was a long and short-haul trucker who transported everything from Campbell's Soup to atomic warheads. He earned about $16,000 a year. One cold day in December 1970, Ray was driving down an icy road in Weed, California when his truck jackknifed. The truck was totaled and Ray was hospitalized for nine days, suffering chronic pain in his neck, left shoulder and back.

But twelve days before the accident, at the urging of a Prudential Insurance Company agent, Ray bought a disability policy which promised to pay $300 a month for fifteen years if he were disabled.

After the accident, doctors prescribed painkillers, tranquilizers, and rest for several months before allowing Ray to return to work. Despite discomfort, Ray began driving again two months later. Then, about a year after his accident, Ray slipped while climbing into the truck's cab. That fall aggravated his injuries and intensified the pain. "I couldn't drive anymore," Ray testified at the trial. "If I turned the steering wheel or depressed the clutch, my left side would go dead on me. I'd lose the grip in my left hand and I would just let go."

Several doctors treated Ray and classified him as disabled. He began receiving his monthly benefits from Prudential, and they continued for about two years. In 1973 Prudential decided to terminate Ray's policy because he was attending a vocational school. Ray protested, and following additional evidence from doctors, Prudential restored his benefits. Except for a minor skirmish in 1976, Prudential paid Ray's disability checks without incident until 1978.

In March 1978, Prudential apparently became impatient with Ray's seemingly slow rehabilitation, although nothing in Ray's policy required him to seek job retraining. In fact, he could have stayed home and vegetated, and the monthly benefits would have been just as payable. Nevertheless, Prudential told Ray that he was no longer totally disabled from any occupation and that his monthly checks would stop. Once again, Ray was faced with a severe loss of income and, once again, he protested.

Finally, in August 1978, Ray was so frustrated that he went to Lee Mandel, a Mount Shasta, California lawyer who wrote a letter on August 10, to Prudential claims adjuster, Jane Garrett informing her that a lawsuit had been filed. On August 24, Garrett wrote back saying that benefits would be restored, and included a check for all amounts due. However, Ray's lawsuit had been filed, and eight months later Prudential filed a countersuit to recover all payments made to Ray as of March 5, 1978. The trial was set for March 18, 1980, in far-off Yreka, California, the seat of Siskiyou County.

In the fall of 1979, Mandel asked me to take over the case and conduct the trial, suggesting that we not let Prudential know until the last minute. Mandel believed that Prudential was not taking the case seriously since the trial would be in a small rural town. The company's $5,000 settlement offer also showed Prudential's lax attitude. We filed a form called an Association of Attorneys on trial day. Prudential's lawyer, John Lynch, from San Francisco, was surprised by this sudden turn of events. His confidence seemed shaken, and he went to the judge's chambers to try to prevent me from coming in as trial counsel. The judge told him that it shouldn't make any difference to Prudential who was trying the case and overruled his objection.

The trial began as scheduled on March 18,1980 in Judge James Kleaver's courtroom. Testimony was taken from eleven witnesses, including Ray, four doctors, Ray's neighbor, a man Ray had worked for, a former state rehabilitation officer, an accountant, and two Prudential employees. We wanted to show an abusive pattern of behavior that started way back in 1973 and was calculated to eliminate Ray's benefits.

On the third day of trial, I called Burdell Benson to the stand as an adverse witness. Benson had worked for Prudential for twenty-five years. He carried the title of claims consultant. He had the Prudential claim file in his hand as he testified about the 1973 incident.

Shernoff: "Now, at this point, did somebody have a question concerning his continuing disability?"

Benson: "Yes, there was a question."

Q. "And did the claims examiner, suggest a complete workup?"

A. "He suggested a workup, yes."

Q. "Complete workup according to the claims file. Did he suggest an interview with the attending physician?"

A. "Yes, he did."

Q. "And what date was that?"

A. "July 18, 1973."

Q. "Now, on July 24th, 1973, was a letter sent to Mr. Pistorius?"

A. "Yes, it was."

Q. "That is approximately six days after the note in the file to have a complete workup and to interview the physician, is that correct?"

A. "Yes."

Q. "In that letter Prudential tells Mr. Pistorius that his benefits are being terminated, is that correct."

A. "Yes, it does."

Q. "This letter was sent to him without any other workup being done, is that correct?"

A. "Correct."

Q. "There was no interview with the physician, is that correct?"

A. "Correct."

Q. "Nothing was done, isn't that correct?"

A. "The decision was made."

Q. "After that, did Mr. Pistorius write a protest letter on August 1, 1973?"

A. "Yes, he did."

Q. "After the protest letter, then Prudential commenced the investigation, did it not?"

A. "Yes."

Q. "Had Mr. Pistorius not complained to Prudential, there would have been no investigation, is that correct.?"

A. "True."

Q. "And he never would have received any more benefits from that date forward, isn't that correct?"

A. "That's true."

I next focused on the 1978 attempt to terminate Ray's benefits. This occurred after a telephone call Prudential made to Ray's treating physician, Roger Howe. Dr. Howe was a young country physician who was well known locally, a competent and friendly man who even made house calls in the Yreka countryside. Dr. Howe testified that Ray was disabled and that he told the Prudential agent during the telephone conversation that Ray's condition was unchanged. I questioned Benson about that call:

Shernoff: "On March 2nd, 1978, the file reflects, does it not, that a Prudential claims adjuster had a telephone conversation with Dr. Howe, is that correct?"

Benson: "Yes."

Q. "And this is in the file on a 'Telephonic Physicians Report?'"

A. "Yes."

Q. "Can you read the handwriting on this?"

A. " 'Last saw March 16, '77. Will be in today (3/1). Secretary will inform insured that I wish to speak to him. Will give him my telephone number and I'll call doctor's office tomorrow for medical info.' "

Q. "Okay. Then on the date of 3/2?"

A. " 'Continuing neck pain. Bothers him while driving. Condition of neck unchanged. Also allergies, blood pressure. Could perform in sedentary occupation with training. No employer would hire him because of a — 'some kind of problem' — 'for any occupation.'

Q. "The file reflected a telephone conversation an adjuster had with Dr. Howe on March 2nd, is that correct?"

A. "Correct."

Q. "Who was the adjuster?"

A. "Frederick Totten."

Q. "On that date did Dr. Howe tell Frederick Totten Mr. Pistorius' condition was unchanged?"

A. "Yes."

Q. "Was there any change in what Dr. Howe told Frederick Totten on that date, over his condition for the last four years?"

A. "Telephone report is basically the same, yes."

Q. "The next thing in the file shows a telephone call from Mr. Pistorius, because, as we saw, there was a request that Mr. Pistorius call, is that correct?"

A. "Correct."

Q. "According to the file, what did Mr. Pistorius tell Mr. Totten when he called in, would you read that to the jury?"

A. "Okay. It's dated 'March 2nd, 1978, notes for file. Mr. Pistorius called me per my request to discuss his claim and was cooperative. Pointed out to him that we had allowed benefits for six-and-a-half years and were concerned with when he might be able to resume work. He related that State Rehabilitation had given him training in the repair of automobile engines and he sought work in this area, but no employer would hire him because he needed a clean bill of health and [attending physician] could not give it to him. He knows of no occupation for which he might be fitted by education, training, or experience which is within his physical capabilities. He said he would like to go back into trucking since he made $2000 a month at that. But in view of insurance [costs] no employer would take the risk of hiring him. He did not finish course on small-engine repair because town already has such a shop—owned by his brother.' Signed by F. Totten."

Q. "So as I understand it, on March 2nd, Mr. Totten talked to both treating doctors and Mr. Pistorius and received the information that was just read to the jury, is that correct?"

A. "Yes."

Q. "The next thing that happened as far as Mr. Pistorius was concerned, on March 8, six days later, his benefits were terminated, is that right?"

A. "Correct."

Q. "You made that decision, didn't you?"

A. "I was one of those that made it, yes."

Q. "And at the time you made that decision, you knew what Dr. Howe said in the telephone conversation just a few days earlier, did you not?"

A. "True."

Q. "You knew what Mr. Pistorius had said, did you not?"

A. "We did."

Q. "Did you have any other additional information at that time, from any other source on March 2nd, March 3rd, March 4th, March 5th, March 6th, or March 7th?"

A. "We had benefit of the entire file."

Q. "At that point in time, if you had any question about his condition of disability, did you have a right under the policy to have him examined by a physician of your own choosing?"

A. "We did."

Q. "You did not elect to do that at that time, did you?"

A. "No, sir. We did not."

Q. "Did you feel terminating his benefits at this time was fair to the insured?"

A. "Absolutely."

When he replied, "Absolutely," we had reached a turning point in the trial. I could start to sense the jurors' anger. The jurors were beginning to get the picture. Prudential tried to terminate Ray's benefits in 1973 without an investigation. They tried again in 1976, until an investigation showed that

Ray was still disabled. Then, in 1978, his treating physician told them that Ray's condition was unchanged. The logical, simply inescapable conclusion was that "unchanged" meant he was still disabled. Dr. Howe said Ray *could* be retrained for a sedentary occupation, but that did not change his disability status.

The jury had already heard Ray's side of the story. He testified that when he was told his benefits would be canceled, he called Prudential immediately and spoke with Frederick Totten in the claims department. Totten told Ray his benefits had been paid for all the years including a period of retraining, and now they would stop—in effect, he told Ray, "Too bad."

Ray asked Totten why Prudential was doing this when his disability was evident and confirmed by his doctors. He asked Totten to arrange for an independent medical examination if the company didn't believe him. Totten contended that the company was not required to do that. Ray told Totten he was going to contact the state Department of Insurance to report Prudential's behavior and, according to Ray's testimony, Totten told him if he did, that Prudential would try to get back the benefits paid for the past six years.

I kept Benson on the stand, building my case largely from his undisguised arrogance and working from the claims file memos.

Shernoff: "In any event, the complaint to the Department of Insurance was received by Prudential and the file reflects that the Department of Insurance asked to see the [Pistorius] file, is that correct?"

Benson: "Yes."

Q. "The file was reviewed with an officer from the Department of Insurance, and a report was in the file, was it not?"

A. "It was."

Q. "In this inspection report, is it true that the Department of Insurance directed Prudential to have an independent medical examination by a physician of their own choosing and to send a copy of the examination report to the Department of Insurance?"

A. "He suggested that we get an examination and that he receive a copy of it"...

Q. "Following that request, Prudential set up an independent medical exam, did it not?"

A. "We do try to cooperate with the commissioner whenever we can, and we did order the exam."

Q. "Does the file reflect the exam being set up?"

A. "Yes."

Q. "Who set up the exam?"

A. "Mr. Totten."

Q. "And on the form who does it say that Mr. Pistorius' treating physician is?"

A. "Dr. Roger Howe."

I knew that Prudential had not been content just to arrange the examination and to let things happen. Prudential actually told the doctor chosen to do the examination that Ray's own physician had not certified his disability and that Ray had been retrained to repair small engines and motors. As the testimony unfolded, it became obvious that both assertions were untrue.

Q. "Now let's get to the special instructions to the doctor."

A. (Reading) " 'We are referring Mr. Pistorius for an independent medical examination to determine if he is totally disabled, unable to perform every occupation for which he is reasonably fitted by education, training or experience. It should be noted that Mr. Pistorius' physician has not certified to his disability. And Mr. Pistorius has been retrained in the repair of small engines and motors.' "

Q. "And this instruction was to be given to Dr. Howland who was selected as the independent medical examiner?"

A. "Yes."

Q. "Do you know who wrote that?"

A. "I would have to assume Mr. Totten wrote that."

Q. "The reference there that Mr. Pistorius' physician had not certified to his disability is totally false, isn't it, sir?"

A. "No, sir."

Q. "Treating physician is Dr. Howe, isn't it?"

A. "Yes."

Q. "Dr. Howe's certification of disability is in the file, is it not?"

A. "It is over a year old at this point in time."

Q. "The telephone conversation was on

March 2nd [1978], wasn't it?"

A. "But he says he has also not seen Mr. Pistorius since March of '77."

By this testimony, Benson virtually conceded that Dr. Howe had certified Ray as disabled. Benson tried to retrieve the situation for Prudential so he came up with the idea that the doctor hadn't seen Ray for a year. But this wasn't true at all. Indeed, Ray had been examined by Dr. Howe the day before the telephone call. This would become obvious from the records, so I decided to see how big a hole Benson would dig for himself:

Shernoff: "Did you not just testify that when Dr. Howe called on March 2nd, even your own file reflects that Mr. Pistorius' condition was unchanged, same as it had been for the last four years. That was your testimony, wasn't it?"

Benson: "That's what he wrote."

Q. "And do you feel that that telephone conversation, as reflected in your own file, justifies a statement to an independent medical examiner that Mr. Pistorius' physician had not certified to his disability?"

A. "It's our opinion and my opinion that when a doctor has not seen a person for a year or a great length of time, he is in no position to determine at that point whether the man is disabled or not."

Q. "Well, why did you call?"

A. "We called him on March 2nd to find out, in our attempt to be fair to Mr. Pistorius."

Q. "In other words, what you were doing here is Prudential's way of being fair to the insured, is that correct?"

A. "I would say so, yes. We try to get the facts."

Q. "Now look at that telephone report... and I'd like you to look at this carefully. 'will be in today, March 1st,' and that Mr. Totten will call back after the examination, on March 2nd. Does it not say that?"

A. "It does."

Q. "And so when Mr. Totten called back on March 2nd, Mr. Pistorius had been there the day before, hadn't he?"

A. "There is nothing there that tells whether he showed for the appointment or not."

Q. "Well, doesn't it say, 'will be in today, March 1st'?"

A. "It does say that."...

Q. "When the doctor called back on March 2nd, indicating that Ray had continuing neck pain that bothers him while driving, condition unchanged, allergies, blood pressure, and the rest, you don't think that he examined him on that date, on March 1st, like the doctor said he did?"

A. "Doesn't say that he did."

Q. "Sir, if a doctor tells you that he's going to examine a patient on March 1st, and the next day you call him back and he starts telling you these diagnoses, don't you assume that he saw him?''

A. "Unless he says that he actually saw him, I would not know."

Q. "You would not know?"

A. "No."

Q. "And this is the way Prudential handles its claims, is that what you're saying? This is standard operating procedure for Prudential?"

A. "We try to get the facts and base our decision on the facts."

Q. "Did you have any information whatsoever that Dr. Howe had not seen him on March 1st, as he said he did?"

A. "No."

By this time Benson was looking very shaken. It seemed time to wrap up.

Shernoff: "Now the note to [Dr. Howland] also stated that Mr. Pistorius had been retrained in small engine repairs, did it not?"

Benson: "Repair of small engines and motors."

Q. "And that's contrary to what Mr. Pistorius related to Mr. Totten in the phone conversation of March 2nd, is it not?"

A. "Said he did not finish the course in small engine repairs."

Q. "So that statement to Dr. Howland is also

false, based on the information that you had at the time?"

A. "Well, we knew he didn't finish the course."

Q. "Was there any medical [information] or documentation in the file which would show he had indeed been retrained for small engine repair and that the retraining was successful?"

A. "No."

Q. "But that's what was related to the doctor, is that right?"

A. "Yes."

Q. "This doctor was a doctor that Prudential chose, is that correct? And Prudential paid for the exam by Dr. Howland?"

A. "Yes."

That was as much mileage out of the letter to Dr. Howland as we were going to get. We turned our attention to Dr. Howland's report to Prudential and Prudential's attempt to turn that report to its advantage. This testimony turned out to include one of the company's biggest and most embarrassing blunders.

Shernoff: "Dr. Howland sent a report of his examination to Prudential, did he not?"

Benson: "He did."

Q. "Can you read this report to the jury?"

A. "Well, they heard it from Dr. Howland."

Q. "Well read it again—the last paragraph of his report as to his disability."

A. [Reading] " 'As to disability, at this time

because of this painful lesion I would say that since this man is trained for auto mechanics, I would feel he could not do anything dealing in auto mechanics. He is trained by experience to be a truck driver, but I would not feel he is satisfactory for truck driving. He is apparently wanting to be a bus driver and indeed he could be a bus driver for two to three hours a day. However, this would imply than simply do the mechanics of driving and would not be available for any emergencies or changing of bus tires, or such things which may or may not come up during the course of driving a bus.' "

Q. "When that report came in did you read it and review it?"

A. "I believe I did."

Q. "Based upon that report did you feel he was qualified for a job as a schoolbus driver?"

A. "I did."

Q. "Even though the doctor was saying that he could not do any emergency work and could only work for a couple hours a day?""

A. "Says 'two to three hours a day,' yes."

Q. "And he said he shouldn't be driving a truck which carries freight or any other type of material, or cargo, right?"

A. "He says, 'I would not feel he is satisfactory for truck driving.' "

> Q. "But you feel he would be satisfactory
> for driving a bus with children on it, is
> that right?"
>
> A. "That is what the doctor told us."

This answer seemed incredulous to me. The doctor hadn't said that at all. School-bus driving was a hazardous chore in Yreka, with its treacherous, winding mountain roads. One would have to be in tiptop condition to drive a school bus in that winter countryside, where chains are required nearly every day. Dr. Howland had said very clearly in his medical report that Ray might be able to drive a bus two or three hours a day, but that he was definitely not fit for any emergencies, tire changing, that sort of thing. He also suggested that because of the numbness in Ray's neck and arms, he might not be able to drive any large vehicle safely.

When Benson told the court that Ray, with all his medical problems, was fit to drive children around in a school bus, I thought the jurors were going to jump out of their seats. Benson had instantly transformed himself from someone who was willing to deprive a disabled person from a meager income, into someone who would put the lives of local school children in jeopardy.

> Shernoff: "Would you like to have Mr. Pistorius
> drive a school bus with your children on
> it, even for two hours a day, sir?"
>
> Benson: "Without seeing the man myself, there is
> no way I could make that deter-
> mination."
>
> Q. "Based on that medical report, sir?"
>
> A. "The doctor says he is capable of driving
> a bus."
>
> Q. "The doctor says he might be able to
> drive a bus from two to three hours a

day; however, he could not handle any emergencies, like changing bus tires or other things which may come up during the regular course of driving a bus. For example, putting chains on, or snow tires. Do you think Mr. Pistorius could do that?"

A. "I don't know."

Q. "Well, did you call the doctor and ask for clarification at this point?"

A. "At this point we did not."

Q. "When this medical report came in it was reviewed by another [Prudential] claims examiner, was it not?"

A. "Yes."

Q. "Jane Garrett?"

A. "Yes."

Q. "And she says, 'IME doctor states insured cannot perform duties of any mechanic's job, even if insured did spend five years in rehabilitation training. If he could not physically perform duties of occupation, it seems we have little alternative but to continue benefits.' Is that her statement to you?"

A. "It's part of it, yes."

Q. " 'Please advise.' "

A. "Right."

Q. "Ms. Garrett looked at the medical report and concluded there was little alternative but to pay the benefits, isn't that right?"

A. "That's what she said."

Q. "You overruled her, didn't you?"

A. "Yes, I did."

Q. "And you overruled her without checking with the doctor for further clarification, is that right?"

A. "I overruled her on the basis of the reports in the file."

Q. "My question was, before you overruled her did you check with the doctor?"

A. "No, sir, I did not check with the doctor."

Q. "That's your own doctor, Dr. Howland, right?"

A. "Yes."

Q. "So on July 13th, 1978, after you overruled Ms. Garrett, a letter was sent that it was the opinion of the doctor who performed the independent medical examination that he was no longer disabled and that benefits would not be resumed, is that right?"

A. "We did say it was the opinion of the physician who performed the independent medical exam, that he could perform occupational duties."

Q. "Who did you have write that letter?"

A. "Jane Garrett wrote the letter."

Although Garrett had concluded that Ray should be paid, Benson overruled her. Furthermore, he did not have the courage to write the letter himself. He ordered Garrett, who was opposed to the denial, do the dirty work. This definitely affected the women on the jury. Benson seemed tired and he wouldn't even look at the jury. To the jury, Benson was Prudential. I could hardly believe my ears as he took the company down with him:

> Shernoff: "Let me ask you this, Mr. Benson: Do you feel this claim was handled fairly by Prudential Insurance Company?"
>
> Benson: "Yes, I do."
>
> Q. "You realize that the law requires you to handle claims in good faith?"
>
> A. "Absolutely."
>
> Q. "You realize that the insured depends upon you to protect his interests?"
>
> A. "Yes."
>
> Q. "Do you feel you protected Mr. Pistorius' interest in this claim?"
>
> A. "I think we did."
>
> Shernoff: "Your Honor, I have nothing further of this witness."

Under cross-examination, Fred Totten's testimony was equally damaging. The questioning began with Prudential's lawyer, John Lynch.

> Lynch: "Mr. Totten, would you state your full name, please?"
>
> Totten: "Charles Frederick Totten."
>
> Q. "Are you presently employed?"
>
> A. "Yes, I am."
>
> Q. "Who are you employed by?"

A. "Prudential Insurance Company."

Q. "How long have you been so employed?"

A. "Since April of 1973."

Q. "In what capacity are you employed?"

A. "Claims approver."

Q. "How long have you been employed in that capacity?"

A. "Almost seven years."

Q. "That's almost all the time that you have been with Prudential?"

A. "That's all the time that I've been with Prudential."

Q. "Have you had any contact with Mr. Pistorius, Mr. Totten?"

A. "Yes, I have."

Q. "Did you have occasion to talk to Mr. Pistorius on the telephone in 1978?"

A. "Yes, I did."

Q. "Did you make a note of that conversation?"

A. "Yes, I did."

Q. "Do you have any recollection of that telephone conversation aside from your notes?"

A. "Very little, except for the notes."

Q. "Would you flip through the file and find your notes in 1978?"

A. "Yes, I have them now."

Q. "Have you had the opportunity to read those notes?"

A. "Yes, I have."

Q. "Does that refresh your recollection as to what transpired then?"

A. "Yes."

Q. "Did you ever tell Mr. Pistorius that if he went to the Department of Insurance that Prudential would seek recovery of everything that had been paid to him?"

A. "Definitely not."

Q. "Did you say anything like that?"

A. "No, I did not."

Q. "Upon what do you base that?"

A. "My recollection of the particular case and the fact that I have never told anyone that if they went to the insurance commissioner we'd attempt to take away or recover any benefits that we have already paid."

Q. "Is there anything in the memo to indicate the nature of the conversation that you had with Mr. Pistorius at that time?"

A. "By nature, it says that he was cooperative, if that's what you mean by nature."

Q. "And what did you mean by that?"

A. "I meant that I asked him questions, he asked me questions. We got along very well."

Q. "Did you mention to him at all at that time that his benefits were to be terminated?"

A. "No, no decision had been made at that time."

Q. "Were you the one that made the decision?"

A. "No, I was not."

Q. "Did you ever have any other telephone calls from Mr. Pistorius?"

A. "Not to my recollection."

Lynch: "That's all I have, thank you."

Totten's testimony was in direct opposition to what Ray had said from the witness stand about Prudential's threat to "recover" back benefits. Indeed Prudential *was* countersuing for back benefits.

I remembered that Totten had used the word "recover" when he wrote an office memorandum after his telephone conversation with Ray and was sure he had forgotten. I asked him to explain what "recover" means in Prudential parlance.

Shernoff: "Mr. Totten, you say you have very little independent recollection of that conversation, is that correct?"

Totten: "Yes, that's correct."

Q. "You say that you would never tell anybody that you [would] attempt to recover benefits?"

A. "I never told any insured that."

Q. "What does the term 'recover' benefits mean?"

A. "It means to take back what was once paid out."

Q. "Now, there is a difference between terminating benefits and recovering benefits, isn't there?"

A. "Yes, there is."

Q. "Terminating means that you're just going to stop the benefits. And recovering means to go back and take what has already been paid, right?"

A. "Yes."

Q. "Now after this phone conversation on March 2nd, there are some internal memos in the file, isn't that correct?"

A. "Yes, there are."

Q. "That last sentence of one memo says, 'I suggest we recover and leave door open if he wishes to contest our action.' Doesn't it say that?"

A. "Yes, it does."

Q. "It uses the term 'recover,' does it not?"

A. "Yes, it does."

Q. "And down here it says Mr. Totten, right?"

A. "Yes, it does."

Q. "That's you, right?"

A. "Yes, it is."

Q. "And it says 'recover'?"

A. "Yes, it does."

Q. "That means go back and get the back payments, doesn't it?"

A. "No, it does not."

Q. "Isn't that what you just told the jury it meant?"

A. "No."

Q. "Well you just told the court and jury in response to my question that the word 'recover' means to go back and get the back payment and the word 'terminate' means to stop the payment. Didn't you testify to that, sir?"

A. "Yes, I did."

Q. "And the Prudential claims file, right after the conversation on March 2nd, says 'recover,' doesn't it?"

A. "Yes, it does."

Q. "It doesn't say 'terminate,' does it? It says 'recover.' "

A. "That's correct."

Q. "That means go back and get the back payments, doesn't it?"

A. "No, it does not."

The jury looked at Totten in bewilderment. As I had done with Benson, I asked Totten how he felt about the Prudential way of doing business.

Shernoff: "Was this claim handled in a standard way by Prudential Insurance Company?"

Totten: "Yes, realizing that we all are human, I'd

> say yes, it was handled in the standard way."

Q. "And in reviewing the file, as a Prudential Insurance examiner, are you proud of the way Prudential handled this claim?"

A. "I think it was handled fairly. I think it was handled competently and professionally."

Q. "Is this the type of fairness that you extend to all of your insureds?"

A. "Yes, it is."

Shernoff: "Thank you."

Now it was time to show the jury Prudential's wealth. As the largest American insurance company, its assets are astounding. To an unsophisticated jury in Yreka, Prudential's wealth was bound to seem unreal, so I sought out a local accountant to explain the company's finances.

We put accountant Michael S. Pavlik, a Yreka resident, on the stand.

Shernoff: "Let me show you the first four pages of the annual financial statement of Prudential Insurance Company of America, as certified by the Insurance Commissioner in this state. Can you tell us, first of all, does the first page there indicate the assets of Prudential Insurance Company?"

Pavlik: "Yes."

Q. "Basically, without a long definition, just tell us what is meant by assets."

A. "Okay. In a financial statement the assets

are the investments, property, cash, stocks and bonds of a company at a certain date and time."

Q. "At the close of 1978, which is reflected by that statement, can you tell the jury what the total assets of Prudential Insurance were?"

A. "The total assets of Prudential were fifty billion dollars."

Q. "Could you put that figure on the board, because I'm going to ask you to do a calculation as to the net worth."

A. "Just in round numbers?"

Q. "Yes."

[Pavlik wrote the figures on the board.]

Q. "Now actually, were the assets $50,000,000,000, or did you leave off some small change?"

A. "They were $50,054,152,491."

Q. "Does the next page show the liabilities?"

A. "Yes, it does."

Q. "Can you tell us what the liabilities were?"

A. "Okay. Liabilities at the end of their year 1978 were $48,024,700,675."

Q. "Knowing that figure then, can you arrive at what is called a surplus, for net worth?"

A. "Yes."

Q. "Okay, can you show us how you arrive at that?"

[Pavlik writes figures on the board.]

Q. "And you have put on the board, two billion dollars, is that correct?"

A. "Right."

Q. "What does the two billion dollars, according to the annual statement, consist of?"

A. "The two billion dollars consists of special contingency reserves and unassigned funds."

Q. "Would this be then, the net worth of the company?"

A. "Yes, it would."

Q. "Now that two billion dollars, tell the jury how many million are in a billion."

A. "Okay. There is one thousand million dollars in a billion."

Q. "So of the two billion dollars, net worth, what would—just so I can understand the numbers, could you put on the board what ten percent of two billion would be?"

[Pavlik marked it on the board.]

Q. "That would be two hundred million dollars?"

A. "Yes."

Q. "And what would one percent of their net worth be?"

A. "Twenty million dollars."

Q. "One percent of their net worth would be $20,000,000, is that correct?"

[Pavlik nodded.]

Q. "Now, does the next page show their income statement for the year 1978?"

A. "Yes, it does."

Q. "And does it show their gross and net income?"

A. "Yes."

Q. "What was their gross income in 1978?"

A. "Their gross income was $11,176,368,543."

Q. "Now, out of the gross income do you then have to—in order to find the net income, do you have to subtract all the expenses that you pay?"

A. "Yes."

Q. "And reserve for claims?"

A. "Correct."

Q. "And did they do that on their financial statement?"

A. "Yes, they did."

Q. "And would you then come out with a net income for the year after deducting all expenses and reserves for claims?"

A. "Correct."

Q. "And what was that figure?"

A. "The net income before dividends and federal income tax was $1,960,496,597."

Q. "Okay, would you put that figure up there?"

[Pavlik marked it on the board.]

Q. "Would you label the top one as gross income?"

[He again marked it on the board.]

Q. "So as I understand it, the net income before dividends and taxes is $1,900,000,000. Is that correct?"

A. "Correct."

The testimony by Pavlik continued, revealing $1.3 billion paid out in dividends and $360 million paid in taxes to show a net income of roughly $270 million.

When it came time to cross-examine the accountant, Prudential's counsel, Lynch, had a tough job on his hands. There was no way he could minimize Prudential's tremendous wealth. And he wanted to get him off the stand quickly. He wisely asked Pavlik only a few questions about what would happen to the company's surplus if Prudential dissolved and dismissed him.

My summation to the jury began early the next day:

Shernoff: "May it please the Court. Ladies and gentlemen of the jury, good morning.

"It is difficult for me to figure out how to start this closing argument, because you have heard the same things I have heard from the witness stand. And I think you must probably have the same feeling inside you after hearing this evidence, that almost anybody would. You twelve people are sitting on a very important case. There are a lot of social ramifications to it. Why this case happened here, under these circumstances, I don't know. Why you people were chosen, I don't know.

"I think as we go through these facts, which I'm going to attempt to do now, you are going to realize you have a very sober job ahead of you. The reason I say that is because this case involves punitive damages. It's a rare kind of case where a civil jury can actually sit in judgement and decide what an appropriate punishment should be for somebody who may be guilty of what the law calls either oppression or fraud or malice."

I then reviewed the testimony in near-chronological order, pointing out Prudential's outrageous conduct by acting first, investigating afterward, and ignoring the investigation if it didn't suit them in order to save some $30,000. I cited statistics from trial exhibits up through 1978 that doctors had certified Ray's total disability and that his attempts to retrain himself should not be held against him.

I recounted the episodes in 1978.

"Now, we come to March of '78. March 2nd, 1978, they make a phone call to Dr. Howe. You recall Dr. Howe, the doctor from Mount Shasta. Very honest doctor, credible doctor, family physician, wants to help people, wants to treat people. Prudential calls him and there is the record of it right in their own claim file. Dr. Howe tells Mr. Totten, 'Ray will be in today, March 1.' There was a phone call on March 1. Prudential left a message with the doctor's office: 'When Mr. Pistorius comes in, have him call us.'

"Their next note in the claim file is March 2nd. This is the picture: the adjuster calls the doctor and the doctor says, 'he'll be in today later on, I'll examine him. Why don't you call back tomorrow. I'll have the complete story for you.' The guy comes in, the adjuster calls back the next day and Dr. Howe tells him: 'Ray is still disabled.' Perhaps in the future he could do some sedentary job with retraining. But no employer would hire him for any occupation requiring physical labor. It's not only in Prudential's own claim file, it's in the doctor's record.

"Can you believe it? Right after they hang up the phone, on the same day, they tell Mr. Pistorius: 'We just talked to Dr. Howe and he says you are not disabled, and we're cutting you off.' Mr. Pistorius tells them that his training hasn't been successful. He explains he did not finish the course on small engine repair, that no doctor would give him a clean bill of health, et cetera, et cetera.' Then Mr. Pistorius says, 'Well, wait a second, at least give me the benefit of the doubt. Pick a doctor of your own choosing. You've got a right under the policy to do it.' Mr. Pistorius says: 'Don't believe Dr. Howe; don't believe all the doctors; don't believe Social Security; don't believe anybody, get your own doctor.' They say, 'Oh, we don't have to examine you.' And then when he says finally, 'I'm going to file a complaint with the Department of Insurance', they tell him, 'You do that and we'll sue you for all the back benefits.' "

I then suggested to the twelve jurors that maybe Prudential thought it was going to get away with treating a policyholder this way.

"Maybe they think juries up in small towns are

dumb. That's what they might think. I don't think that. I think people are people. People, in Yreka, or L.A., or Chicago, anywhere, don't like to be cheated. There is no such thing as a dumb jury and Prudential is going to find that out."

The company's arrogance made me especially angry.

"Do they have the courage and the decency to come into this courtroom and say, 'that's bad, that was a mistake. We're a proud company. We shouldn't really be doing things like that.' No. They take the oath and they say, 'that's fair. That's the way we handle claims.' I wouldn't have believed it unless I heard it."

Finally, I talked about damages. I explained that Ray was entitled to the cash value of his policy: $17,200, I also pointed out that Ray had suffered so much from humiliation and anger that an old ulcer started acting up. Ray had been hospitalized for fear he was having a heart attack. I recounted Ray's financial woes, explaining how he had had to borrow money and that his credit cards had been canceled. Translating Ray's mental distress into money was difficult.

"It's a subjective thing. The law doesn't give any fixed standard or guidance or formula. I think if I had to give you some guidance, I'd figure somewhere between $10,000 and $50,000. Some of you might think higher, some of you might think lower. Nobody can argue with it, really."

It was the punitive damages issue, though, that allowed me to say what I really wanted to. I explained to the jury that the law says that deterrence and punishment have little effect if the wealth of the defendant allows it to absorb the amount of the damages with no discomfort. I wanted the jury to make the award a little bit uncomfortable for

Prudential.

I pleaded with the jury to take a good look at the evidence, specifically the company's annual report as it was explained by the accountant.

> "After they pay all their expenses; after they pay all their dividends; after they've reserved for all claims; even after they pay their income taxes, their net income is $270 million per year, or approximately $5 million per week, or approximately a million dollars a day. That's profit. That is what is left after they pay all their expenses. A million dollars a day."

I pointed out that a court would certainly not hesitate to fine a few days' pay if an individual had swindled $30,000. Or what about the company surplus—a surplus of over $2 billion. A court would find nothing wrong with fining an ordinary individual criminal one percent of his surplus.

Then, after I had explained the figures and repeated my philosophy of punishment and deterrence, I ended my summation with my customary tone:

> "I think I have really talked long enough. I think I have done my job. That's all I can do. I can subpoena the records. I can bring them into this courtroom. I can put Prudential on the witness stand. I can expose everything. I can let you see it. I can let you hear it. I can let you feel it. And my job is done. In a few minutes it's going to be your job. You are going to have to talk to that company. You are going to have to speak for Mr. Pistorius and for all the people, because punitive damages involve society. You are going to be talking with this verdict."

Lynch's argument was a painstaking recitation of medical details and other irrelevant information. At 8:30 P.M., March 25, 1980, after about six hours of deliberation, a jury of conservative rural California railroad and lumber people came in with an astounding verdict. Ray was awarded compensatory damages for his mental distress of $45,000. Then the jury socked Prudential with a $1 million punitive damage award. It was the largest punitive award ever assessed against Prudential on behalf of a policyholder.

Judge Kleaver rejected Prudential's motion for a new trial. Prudential appealed, claiming that the amount of the award was excessive. Even the Court of Appeals upheld the $1 million award and concentrated, just like the jury, on Prudential's misrepresentations of facts and on the company's courtroom concession that it was standard procedure to cut off disability payments and not reinstate them unless the policyholder complained. In an opinion notable for its simplicity, the three appellate judges concluded that there was:

> "no doubt concerning the existence of substantial evidence of emotional distress, consisting of anger, anxiety, humiliation and frustration, due to actions of defendant."

The court also concluded that Prudential acted, at the very least, with a conscious disregard of Pistorius's rights and he was therefore entitled to punitive damages. As for the punitive damages, the judges justified the amount and wrote:

> "For the year 1978, defendant's net income after taxes and dividends was $270 million. Its gross assets were in excess of $50 billion and its net worth $2 billion. The award of $1 million was thus .00002 percent of its gross assets. And it was approximately one-twentieth of 1 percent of its net worth."

Summing up the presentation of facts in the case, the judges made note of numerous misrepresentations and irregularities and then wrote:

> "Defendant repeatedly testified its handling of the

claim was proper and in accordance with its standard operating procedures, it handled this claim fairly, it handled all its claims in the same fashion as it handled this one, and it would handle plaintiff's claim the same way if it had to do it all over again."

Prudential's petition to the California Supreme Court was denied and the case was over. Shortly thereafter, Prudential paid the full amount plus interest. Ray Pistorius truly did get a piece of the rock.

# Chapter 7

# Are We All Being Overcharged?

Americans spend 12 cents out of every dollar for insurance, yet many do not know how insurance rates are set. Most people assume that a government agency like a public utility commission must approve insurance rate increases. However, many states have no rate-making regulations. In California, for example, insurance companies can charge whatever they please. Although a number of states do require their departments of insurance to review rate hikes, most have neither the incentive nor the expertise to do the job in a way that guarantees public protection.

The insurance industry has always argued that competition will keep rates down. But this free market philosophy can work only if there is an informed consumer population and there is no such thing in the insurance business. Comparison shopping among insurance companies is almost impossible. Insurance companies purposely set premiums and describe benefits so that comparisons are difficult. No two policies are alike. Companies do not use new technology which could provide consumers with access to a central listing of insurance prices, and few consumers can take the time to contact all the companies that offer comparable coverage. Perhaps someday consumers will be able to call the insurance agent for rates, coverage, and carriers much as travelers can call travel agents for prices, flights, and airlines.

I suspect that most Americans have the uneasy feeling they are usually being overcharged for their insurance coverage. I think they are probably right. And there is a way of fighting back. One group of angry insurance consumers challenged an insurance company successfully on the question of excessive rates.

The Southern California Physicians Council (SOCAP) represents thousands of doctors. It was this group that led the fight against sky-high medical malpractice insurance rates. SOCAP's president was dynamic doctor Edward Zalta, who could have doubled as a lawyer. One of his colleagues described him "as a real sweet guy at heart, even if he does have the personality of a buzz saw."

One unusually quiet day, I was sitting at my desk when the phone rang. It was Dr. Zalta. He started right in trying to convince me that Travelers Insurance Company had overcharged SOCAP doctors grossly on their insurance premiums and he wanted to sue. At the time, it seemed most strange. To my knowledge, no one had ever sued an insurance company for charging too much. It was commonplace to sue them over claims, but to attack them for excessive premiums was something else again. Ed Zalta was so enthusiastic that I thought I should get involved— just so that some of his energy would rub off on me.

The saga began in 1973, when the Hartford Insurance Group was negotiating a new contract with SOCAP. Hartford wanted a rate hike of 100 percent, and negotiations broke down. About this time Travelers entered the picture, apparently to increase its involvement in the medical-malpractice insurance market.

Travelers won SOCAP away from Hartford by offering an increased premium of only 30 percent and by adding something called a "rate-stabilization fund." Travelers' contract stated if premiums in any given year exceeded the cost of covering claims, the cost of administration, and a reasonable profit for Travelers, the excess money would go into a fund to be credited against future premiums. (The provision, however, did not make clear what would happen to the money in the fund if Travelers terminated its contract with SOCAP.) SOCAP signed up with Travelers and had a three-year period of relative peace.

Then, in 1976, Travelers demanded a 486 percent rate increase, claiming high losses on malpractice policies past, present, and future. The doctors were dumbfounded. They fought the increase with little success, and Travelers finally imposed a 327 percent hike. Zalta denounced this rate, calling it "obscene." Premiums doubled and tripled and several neurosurgeons and orthopedic surgeons received bills for over $35,000 per year for their malpractice premiums. A number of doctors left the state; others even quit practice. Many participated in a doctor's strike, an event that brought national publicity, as well as some bumper-sticker humor. Bumper stickers on cars up and down the state read: "Feeling sick? Call your lawyer."

The increase that Travelers demanded, based on alleged losses, made doctors very suspicious. The relationship between SOCAP and the insurance company deteriorated seriously. Travelers decided to end its venture into California medical malpractice insurance by canceling the SOCAP contract upon its expiration in 1978. When this happened, Zalta decided to look into Travelers' profit picture and into the rate-stabilization fund. He thought the company might owe the doctors a substantial amount of money.

The rate-fund provision read:

> "The responsibility for the administration of the fund rests with Travelers. The disposition of the fund may take the form of credits to future rates or premiums, or other similar form agreed to by SOCAP and Travelers, provided that no one other than Travelers shall have the right to or interest in such fund except as it may affect future premiums for insurance."

At first it seemed unequivocal. Travelers controlled the

fund, and that was that. However, I thought the clause was subject to various interpretations. The clause was vague. I felt that the doctors would have a reasonable chance of winning a case against Travelers and I was especially interested in whether there were excess profits. If that turned out to be the case, why did the company create such a fuss? I began to wonder whether it really needed to hike premiums so drastically in the first place.

Zalta and his SOCAP colleagues began digging into all available statistics on Travelers' performance during the five years of the SOCAP contract. After meticulous research and persistent questioning, it became clear that 1976, 1977, and 1978 were highly profitable years for Travelers Insurance Companies. When the SOCAP team had gathered enough evidence to show that millions of dollars were in question, Zalta confronted Travelers. He wanted to know just how much money the company would disburse from the rate-stabilization fund.

According to Zalta, Travelers' first response was "What fund?" Then, as Zalta tells it, "After a long period of dilly-dallying, Travelers began stonewalling us. One of its people said, 'That money belongs to us.' Another Travelers official said, 'We don't owe you a dime.' " Travelers officials denied making those statements.

After the intial stonewalling, Zalta's persistence paid off. Travelers finally agreed to negotiate with SOCAP. After a series of bitter exchanges, Travelers eventually conceded that there was some money in the rate-stabilization fund, and that the doctors might have a right to some of the fund. Travelers offered SOCAP an $11 million first payment, with additional payments over the next ten years, depending on claims experience. The total was about $36 million. That offer did not excite Ed Zalta. He wanted interest paid on premiums held, and he wanted more participation in the Travelers' excess profits. He said, "They had collected over $131 million in premiums, and paid out less than 25 percent of that in losses. In short, Travelers had taken our money, used it interest-free, and intended to return only a discounted portion to us after inflation had eroded its value. We said, 'To hell with that.' "

SOCAP's patience with Travelers began wearing thin. They decided that they had better contact a law firm to prepare a lawsuit if no better offer was forthcoming. However, the doctors made one last stab at settling the matter themselves. They decided to seek a high-level meeting. Travelers agreed. That meeting took place in Hartford, Connecticut, Travelers' home city. No attorneys were present. It was simply a last-ditch negotiating effort between Travelers' officials and SOCAP's officials. After the meeting, Zalta and the rest of the SOCAP staff felt they had made good progress. They believed Travelers had agreed that the premiums imposed in 1976 were excessive, and that the rate-stabilization fund would be studied closely. Best of all, Travelers had promised to respond soon with a more favorable offer.

Days and weeks passed, and no offer was forthcoming. Officials at SOCAP began to panic because there was some uncertainty about whether the statute of limitations would run out on the Travelers' contract, thereby precluding any possible lawsuit. The deadline was less than a month away, and SOCAP either had to strike a deal with Travelers or file a lawsuit. Just a few days before the statute of limitations would run out, Travelers sent an extremely disappointing Telex message to SOCAP leaders. Zalta recalls, 'Some of us started pounding the walls in anger and frustration. Others went into deep depression. The offer was an insult." The offer fell far short of the previous offer, which had been based on an initial payout of $11 million. The new offer started with an initial payment of only $6 million.

SOCAP leaders held an emergency meeting to review the situation. They had already spent $100,000 on this dispute and were told by their regular association lawyer that

$600,000 more would be needed to prosecute a case in court. SOCAP could not afford that large an outlay. Besides, they knew that there was always a risk a jury could end up on Travelers' side. According to Zalta, their association lawyer advised them to accept the offer. It was at this point that Zalta called me, imploring me to file a lawsuit against Travelers immediately. It occurred to me that doctors and lawyers rarely get together on anything. Now, for the first time, we would be able to work together against the insurance industry.

Zalta let me take charge immediately. I practically dropped everything to begin working nonstop on SOCAP's problem. A lawsuit was filed within twenty-four hours. The lawsuit included a demand for the return of all excess premiums, plus other damages. We also threw in a demand for $1 billion in punitive damages for good measure.

Travelers' reaction was swift, and as Zalta expressed it later, "as though they'd been goosed. They leaped across the country to Los Angeles and diligently resumed negotiations with us. Travelers representatives began conducting marathon negotiations. Role reversal became the order of the day. Where we had waited patiently for them to return our calls and letters, they were now awaiting ours."

This time, the negotiations involved actuaries, SOCAP officials, Travelers officials, a highly respected and able Travelers lawyer by the name of George A. McKeon, and me. McKeon was bright and fair. I felt from the beginning that he wanted to get this matter behind Travelers and did not want any part of the lawsuit. I told McKeon that we would be willing to negotiate further, so long as we felt there was good progress being made. If this did not work, we would pursue our lawsuit swiftly and zealously. It became increasingly clear to me that Travelers wanted to settle. The company made all of its records available to us, including its actuarial statistics and projections. A very complicated formula was worked out by which SOCAP and Travelers would share in the excess profits that had been made to date, and would also share in excess profits made in the future.

After several months of intensive negotiations, a settlement was reached. Travelers agreed to pay an initial refund of $18.6 million. Further refunds, depending on future claims payouts, would follow each year for ten years. Any money remaining in the fund after ten years would go to SOCAP. The settlement had an estimated value of between $50 million and $61 million, according to the best projections that could be made from Travelers' actuarial statistics. The refunds would be shared by about 5,500 doctors who were policyholders and SOCAP members. The settlement made big news in the papers and on television across the country. This was the first time an insurance carrier had been forced to return excess premiums.

The case not only never went to trial, it really never got off the ground. I did more negotiating than I did lawyering, and in the process I learned a lot about how insurance rates are set. From what I learned, it was pretty easy to conclude that insurance consumers of all kinds are prey to this sort of action and are in need of protection. Certainly if doctors could be overcharged, less-powerful consumers are even more vulnerable.

One interesting by-product of the doctors' crisis was the fact that the doctors also complained to the state legislature about the drastic increase in their insurance rates. The legislature responded by passing the Medical Injury Compensation Reform Act, effectively making it harder for victims of malpractice to sue their doctors and collect. The end result was that valuable consumer rights were taken away by this legislative action, all brought about by the drastic increases in insurance rates that turned out to be not so justified.

Today, years after SOCAP's dramatic rate increases were shown to be unnecessary, the same song is being replayed across the country but to an even wider audience. Property and casualty insurance rates (for even more limited coverage) are going through the roof. The insurance industry's public relation mills are blaming lawyers and juries. This is nonsense! A full and fair investigation would undoubtedly reveal many other causes for any temporary dip in their usual handsome profit picture. Exorbitant rate increases are not necessary. Profits (for property and casualty companies) are already beginning to soar. The chart below says it all. Tremendous profits are being made and hardly any taxes are being paid. Yet, the insurance industry's public relation mills grind on to make it sound like the insurance industry is really hurting. They blame everyone in sight for increased premiums and seem to want to keep secret the real profits they are making.

But nobody investigates the sacred insurance industry— that sacred cow that gives off a lot of sacred bull. The worst part of our current crisis is that the insurance industry is trying to spread the word that cutting away citizens' rights (so-called tort reform) will solve the rate problem and lower premiums. If you believe that story, you might as well believe in the tooth fairy. I believe the only result of curtailing citizens' rights to sue will be to increase the insurance industry's profits even more dramatically. We need Insurance Reform, not reform of our civil justice system. Insurance companies should have to justify their rate increases to a truly objective governmental tribunal (much as a public utility has to do). This would guaranty those companies a fixed rate of return, but no more. If this were ever put into effect, insurance premiums would come down drastically.

I believed that random lawsuits would not solve the excess-rate problem, but what was needed was a national organization to protect insurance consumers. At about the

| Name of Insurance Company | 1986 Net Income | 1986 Federal Taxes Incurred | Surplus As of 12/31/86 |
|---|---|---|---|
| State Farm Mutual | $ 1,615,655,155 | –0– | $ 12.1 Billion |
| Aetna Life & Casualty | 1,013,771,074 | –0– | 3.5 Billion |
| Allstate Insurance Co. | 656,541,268 | –0– | 4.1 Billion |
| Hartford Fire Ins. Co. | 542,851,117 | –0– | 2.3 Billion |
| Amer. Int'l Group, Inc. | 525,719,783 | –0– | 2.9 Billion |
| Liberty Mutual Ins. Co. | 454,899,721 | –0– | 1.8 Billion |
| Ins. Co. of North America | 454,103,785 | –0– | 1.4 Billion |
| United States Auto Assn. | 369,640,282 | –0– | 1.7 Billion |
| Travelers Indemnity Co. | 306,749,373 | –0– | 2.9 Billion |
| Crum & Forster Ins. Cos. | 241,979,607 | –0– | 1.1 Billion |
| U.S. Fidelity & Guar. Co. | 218,009,304 | –0– | 1.2 Billion |
| Lumbermens Mut. Casualty | 201,449,615 | –0– | 1.1 Billion |
| Safeco Ins. Co. of America | 159,342,578 | –0– | 622 Million |
| Ohio Casualty Ins. Co. | 139,781,320 | –0– | 452 Million |
| Continental Casualty Co. | 359,141,107 | 1,019,038 | 1.8 Billion |
| St. Paul Fire & Marine Ins. | 230,150,437 | 2,039,850 | 942 Million |
| Home Insurance Co. | 199,158,152 | 5,331,045 | 770 Million |
| Continental Insurance Co. | 272,778,921 | 13,778,687 | 1.3 Billion |
| Chubb (Fed. Insurance Co.) | 244,281,988 | 14,220,334 | 982 Million |
| Firemans Fund Insurance Co. | 351,306,397 | 44,125,402 | 1.3 Billion |

NOTE: A sample of 20 property and casualty companies. Figures taken from official Financial Statements on file with the California Department of Insurance. Consolidated reports used where appropriate. Net income includes Federal Tax refunds.

time I was negotiating the SOCAP settlement, I became
friendly with Ralph Nader. We both happened to be in San
Francisco soon after the SOCAP settlement, and he asked
me about the case. I bent his ear for over an hour on the
whole problem of the insurance consumer. He said that he,
too, had been considering a national group, but had put the
idea aside because he could not think of a qualified person
to lead such a group.

By another lucky coincidence, at about this same time,
Robert Hunter, former head of the Federal Insurance
Administration, was considering leaving government
service. Bob Hunter is an actuary who had been working for
insurance companies for years before joining the federal
government. His knowledge in the private and public sector
is unmatched, and he was a friend of Nader's. Ralph told me
about him, and even though I had never met an actuary I
liked, I was willing to meet and talk with Hunter. His
knowledge of the industry was impressive, and his
dedication to the consumer was obvious immediately. I
recall the following story he told me:

> "My father was in insurance and I remember when I
> was little he used to say all the time that insurance
> was a business of utmost good faith. His particular
> work was in marine insurance, and I can remember
> very clearly during the war the kind of faith people
> had. There was a tremendous effort then for ships to
> hug the coast to avoid enemy submarines and in one
> instance a ship ran aground somewhere in Nova
> Scotia. My father wired London [where most of the
> underwriters were], explaining that damages were
> somewhere around $6 million and that he needed $3
> million immediately. London wired the money right
> back. All they needed was my father's word. I was
> impressed by that. I grew up believing insurance
> was an idealistic business. I saw my father making
> decisions based on what he thought was morally

right. Insurance should be an idealistic business, but
it's not."

Hunter was perfect for the job, and the National
Insurance Consumer Organization (NICO) was formed as a
nonprofit consumer organization that studies insurance
issues on behalf of consumers. Hunter enlisted Howard
Clark and James Hunt, former state insurance
commissioners in South Carolina and Vermont,
respectively, to be directors of NICO. These three men are
rare examples of consumer-oriented officials. They know
insurance inside-out and they provide NICO with the
expertise necessary to combat the insurance industry's
effective propaganda mills.

Since its creation, NICO has been a vigorous consumer
supporter. It has done everything from testifying before
Congress to lending a hand to disgruntled policyholders.
NICO has been especially interested in insurance rate-
making practices. According to Bob Hunter, "Rate-making
practices are antiquated and ludicrous." His study, "Taking
the Bite Out of Insurance," on private-passenger-car
insurance prices and a later report on rate making in the
property and casualty insurance industry, support this
accusation. For example, most states ignore insurance
company investment income (as part of its profitability) in
rate-making regulation.

Hunter's reports made it obvious that failing to consider
investment income in rate setting is an outrageous affront
to insurance consumers. Hunter claims, "Income from
investments now greatly exceeds income from premiums in
most lines of insurance. To omit investment income from
the total profit picture—the picture the rate makers use to
set premium rates—is doubly bad for the consumer. It
doesn't take a genius to figure out that if you take a dollar
from someone and give him back ninety-five cents a year
later, your profit on the transaction is five cents plus

whatever you gained from using the dollar for a year."

Insurance companies in most states still have the luxury of operating under a standard set in 1921, when the National Convention of Insurance Commissioners specified a 5 percent profit formula. The convention ignored investment income as a factor in figuring profit. The theory was and is that competition in the industry would keep premium rates in line. Twenty years later, the Supreme Court ruled that insurance companies were subject to federal antitrust laws. But the law was soon invalidated when Congress passed the McCarran-Ferguson Act, exempting the insurance industry from antitrust liability. Regulation of insurance sales practices and rate standards was left to the states, and it is no secret that all but a handful of insurance regulators are former insurance industry personnel.

In his very readable and informative book, *The Invisible Bankers*, Andrew Tobias writes in the chapter "How God Would Restructure the Insurance Industry":

> "In North Carolina, in 1981, three of the eleven members of the Senate Insurance Committee owned and operated insurance agencies. A fourth was a director of Columbus Standard Life. In the House, four of seventeen committee members owned and operated insurance agencies; two more were lawyers representing insurance companies."

He also notes a General Accounting Office study that found "serious shortcomings" in the way states were regulating insurance. "Insurance regulation," said the GAO, "is not characterized by an arm's-length relationship between the regulators and the regulated." The insurance industry has been nearly 100 percent successful in keeping investment income out of the rate-making process. Hunter is an exceedingly articulate spokesman for the consumer.

He has involved himself so effectively in insurance consumer advocacy that in the first three years there were 30 stories quoting NICO in *The New York Times,* as well as in hundreds of other dailies and weeklies: He has appeared several times on the "Today," Donahue, and Mike Douglas shows. Hunter considers all this media attention as a sign that NICO's work is having some effect:

> "There are two million insurance employees the press can use, and who is the other side? We are. We're it. And we've been right so many times the media has grown to trust us. So has Congress, and I testify before committees all the time. When we put out a study, for example, on how factoring investment income to workers compensation insurance would lower premium rates by about 20 percent, the industry claimed we were wrong. Of course, we were proved right when GAO analyzed it and that gave us credibility. The same thing proved true over auto insurance rates, and every time that happens, we become more effective."

NICO has successfully intervened in several state and federal matters, including:

1. The *Norris* unisex case in the Supreme Court. The Court ruled in favor of the Arizona employee who was demanding equal pay-in and pay-out for men and women in pension plans.

2. Auto insurance rates. NICO testified before Congress on why mileage—and not gender—is a relevant criterion in determining premiums.

3. Anticompetitive behavior in rate making. NICO's documentation helped convince Congress to order a Government Accounting Office study on state regulation of insurance.

Nothing has been too small or unimportant for NICO. That's what I like about Hunter and the organization. For example, NICO intervened in New Mexico to help prove that auto insurance rates were higher in Indian areas than in non-Indian areas. That practice and overcharging in general was corrected for automobile insurance throughout New Mexico.

Another good example is the case of Daisy Cook, who had taken out an accidental death policy on her grandson's life. She paid Commonwealth Life Insurance Company ten cents a week for 19 years. Kino Lewis, her grandson, was shot and killed in a random racial murder. When Cook tried to collect her $1,500, Commonwealth Life wrote her back and enclosed a check for 80 cents—a refund for eight weeks of excess premiums. Commonwealth told the dead man's grandmother that the policy did not pay for "any loss resulting from…injuries intentionally inflicted upon the insured by any person other than burglars or robbers."

In March of 1982, three months after her grandson was killed, Cook asked NICO for help. NICO was given the runaround by the carrier and was refused assistance by the Indiana Insurance Commissioner. Hunter took the story to Jack Anderson, who ran a column on the abusive treatment. The column inspired hundreds of letters and telephone calls to Cook and to the newspapers.

Even though Commonwealth Life denied that the public pressure had anything to do with deciding to pay the claim, Commonwealth Life hand-delivered a check to Daisy Cook one week after the Anderson column ran. Hunter says "NICO has yet to see an insurer pay a claim it did not feel it legally had to."

NICO has had a significant impact on the insurance industry at every level. Hunter is tireless in his pursuit of fair insurance practices, and he intends to keep on going until he retires, about fifteen years down the road. But, he says, when he does bow out, he's going to Tahiti. "There's no word for insurance in the Tahitian language," he reports.

# Chapter 8

# Metropolitan Life
# and Death

In life insurance, there should be little room for argument. The company pays upon death, and deciding whether the policyholder is dead or alive should be easy to figure out even for the most combative insurance companies. In disability insurance, an argument may arise over whether a person is disabled; fire insurance companies may dispute the amount of damage; medical insurers may argue over what is covered and what is not. With life insurance, once the company is presented with the death certificate, it should pay.

But it doesn't always work out that way. Life insurance companies have found a way to complicate matters. Many life policies have double-indemnity provisions: this means the beneficiary will be paid double if the policyholder meets with an accidental death. Often a controversy develops over the definition of accidental death, and it is these controversies that expose life insurance to the world of bad faith.

*Mary Frazier* v. *Metropolitan Life Insurance Company* was a bad faith case if ever I saw one. The amount of the double-indemnity provision was $12,000.

Mary's battle with Metropolitan began after her twenty-three-year-old husband David drowned on March 13, 1975. David and Mary had been married happily for five years, and they had one child. His postal service employee benefits included a $12,000 double-indemnity life insurance policy. According to the policy, the widow expected $24,000.

The Frazier family was close, and David, his brother, Curtis, and their mother, Mae, liked to go fishing near the Channel Islands, about 75 miles up the coast from Los Angeles. One day Mae talked her two sons into accompanying her on a trip out to the islands on the *Electra*, a fishing vessel she liked and had been on before. The *Electra* left the harbor at night and by morning was in place for fishing.

Sixty passengers were aboard, and most fished the entire day before the *Electra* headed back to the harbor in the early evening. As the boat entered Channel Island Harbor in Ventura County, David was walking near the outside rail. Suddenly he was in the water. Mae, who was in the boat's cabin, said she saw him fall over backward into the water. Crew members claimed that David screamed, "Don't let them get me!" and jumped overboard.

There was some confusion about what happened after he hit the water. Some crew members claimed that he resisted rescue by swimming away from the boat. Mae Frazier remembered clearly that she had shouted to David, screaming to him to swim away from the boat toward the rocks, about 75 feet away. No one disputed that David was treading water for a while before he disappeared beneath the surface and drowned.

Metropolitan paid Mary Frazier the first $12,000 of the death benefit and then refused to pay the double-indemnity payment of $12,000. A claims representative wrote Mary and told her that the company had made a thorough investigation of the events and concluded that David had committed suicide.

This was news to his widow because Mary knew that her husband was not suicidal. She told Metropolitan that she and David were regular churchgoers, and suicide was contrary to their religion. Indeed, Mary was so disturbed by the allegations of suicide and so embarrassed that she felt compelled to leave Los Angeles and find refuge with relatives in Kansas. When she returned five months later to place flowers on her husband's grave in honor of Memorial Day, she decided that the stigma of suicide was too great to bear and that the family name had to be cleared. She engaged the services of attorney Hal B. Williams, Jr., one of Los Angeles's finest personal injury lawyers.

Williams brought a suit against the owners of the *Electra.* He claimed that debris on the deck may have caused David's fall into the sea and that the crew failed to use proper manoverboard and rescue procedures. The negligence trial took place in 1978, and a Ventura County Superior Court found the boat crew had been negligent and their negligence caused David's death. They awarded Mary damages for David's death and, with this money, Mary paid for her training as a dental technician.

The second lawsuit, the bad faith case against Metropolitan, was filed later, but did not come to trial until four years after Mary had won her negligence case. I was now on the case, and the issues were clear to us. I was really confident about the suit because we had such strong evidence. Two key documents—one an internal Metropolitan memo and the other a letter sent by the insurance company to its investigators—would give the jury a textbook definition of bad faith.

The internal memo was written by Claims Supervisor Charles Pfaffenbach, who died before the case came to trial. He would not be able to explain the memo dated February 19, 1976, *one day before* Mary Frazier was informed by Metropolitan that because of the company's suicide finding, she was not eligible for the $12,000 accidental-death benefit.

Pfaffenbach wrote the memo to his boss, Albert Danz, assistant manager in charge of claims. It said:

> *"I still doubt we could sustain a denial in court. Unless you want to deny now [and] try for a compromise later when she complains."*

That memo meant one thing: Pfaffenbach had reviewed

all the evidence, decided the claim was payable, and
admitted that any denial would not hold up in court. The
memo was dynamite—and I knew what I could do with it in
front of a jury.

Danz's written response was:

*"Deny, refer any protests [to me]."*

I knew when I first saw this memo that it would be the
focus of the trial. No matter what Metropolitan tried to do,
nor how hard the company lawyers tried to divert the
jurors' attention from the memo, those handwritten words
would demonstrate Metropolitan's bad faith.

A letter from Metropolitan to Retail Credit, an
investigating firm that worked closely with insurance
companies, was one more nail in the coffin. When I first
looked at it, it seemed innocuous enough. Then I took a
second look. The concluding sentence read:

"As it would appear that the insured attempted
suicide. We would appreciate a full report of
investigation concerning any motive for suicide."

It then seemed to me that Metropolitan was actually
asking Retail Credit *to find* motives for *suicide.* Period. The
end.

The trial began February 15, 1983, in the Los Angeles
Superior Court, with the honorable M. Ross Bigelow
presiding. Hal Williams represented Mary Frazier. He had
asked me to join him as our combined experience—his
intimate knowledge of the case and my bad faith practice—
made a strong team.

Metropolitan was defended by Adams, Duque &
Hazeltine, a Los Angeles firm that had represented many
insurance companies in bad faith actions. James Willcox
was their team leader.

I had hoped that we would be able to use the results of the
earlier negligence lawsuit against the *Electra* owners to
show that a jury had already decided that David's death was

accidental. However, Judge Bigelow ruled that since Metropolitan had not been a part of the earlier lawsuit, nothing from that case could be brought into this trial because suicide had not been an issue in the negligence suit. His ruling lengthened the trial considerably, even though it had been established in another court at another time exactly what happened on the boat the day of David's death.

In another ruling, the judge decided he wanted Metropolitan's liability established before the jury determined appropriate damage amounts. He split the trial in two: bifurcating, in legal parlance. The cause of death, the insurance company's liability, and the extent of the liability would be determined first. Following jury decisions on those issues, appropriate amounts for mental and emotional distress and punitive damages would then be decided.

The questions that had to be answered during the first phase of the trial were:

> One: Did David Frazier's death result from accidental means?
>
> Two: Did Metropolitan violate its duty of good faith and fair dealing in investigating and then denying the claim?
>
> Three: Did Metropolitan's conduct amount to malice, oppression or fraud?

We contended that Metropolitan had no evidence to support suicide. Whatever the conflicting testimony was—from David's relatives on the boat, from members of the crew, or from other passengers—bottom line was that David had no cause to commit suicide. He had never indicated he was suicidal and had never behaved in an aberrant way—I was certain of this. I was just as certain that Metropolitan had violated its duty of good faith, but those legal issues were more complex.

Metropolitan's major witness on the bad faith issue was Albert Danz, a nice, grandfatherly man who made a good impression on the stand. Since the time he wrote his note, he had retired from Metropolitan. He was knowledgeable and cooperative as Willcox, the Metropolitan attorney, led him through the Frazier file step by step. It was becoming obvious that Metropolitan's strategy was to have Danz explain away the company's handling of the case.

Danz said that it was Pfaffenbach who had doubts about the cause of David's death. On the witness stand, Danz said he reviewed the file independently and made the final decision to deny the claim. In other words, the memo was not indicative of Danz's state of mind, but only of the late Pfaffenbach's, whose state of mind was now out of the reach of mortal man. I had a hunch that Danz's story would fall apart if I cross-examined him properly. He appeared to be an honest man, and I believed he would give honest responses to straightforward questions.

I started by calling his attention to the letter his company had written to Retail Credit to commence the investigation. I was certain that Danz hadn't looked carefully at this letter and was unaware of its significance.

> Shernoff: "To your knowledge, sir, isn't it true that Retail Credit is a firm that performs investigative services for insurance companies?"
>
> Danz: "Yes, sir."
>
> Q. "Before Metropolitan Life Insurance had Retail Credit do any investigation whatsoever, didn't Metropolitan Life Insurance already conclude that this death was apparently due to suicide?"
>
> A. "I would say no."
>
> Q. "Would you please turn to document 65?"

A. "You want document no. 65?"

Q. "Yes, document 65. If I may just look over your shoulder, sir."

A. "Sure."

Q. "Isn't that the very first letter to Retail Credit asking them to do an investigation?"

A. "I believe so. Let me just check. Yes, sir."

Q.: "This letter was actually directing Retail Credit to do an investigation; was it not?"

A. "Yes, sir."

Q. "And at this time you had in the file what had been sent by Mrs. Frazier; is that correct?"

A. "I believe so."

Q. "Now, directing your attention to the last paragraph of your letter—Metropolitan's letter to Retail Credit—isn't it true in fact —that in the last paragraph, it says, 'It would appear that the insured attempted suicide. We would appreciate a full report of [the] investigation concerning any motive for suicide?'"

A. "Oh, yes."

Q. "Isn't it true, now that you have reviewed that letter, even before any investigation was done that Metropolitan informed Retail Credit that Metropolitan felt that this was probably a suicide and that they should get the motives for suicide?"

A. "Well, it does state, 'It would appear,' and, 'We would appreciate a full report of investigation concerning any motive for suicide,' et cetera."

Q. "Let me ask you this: If you're going to ask somebody to do an investigation for you, don't you want to have full and fair investigation?"

A. "Yes, sir."

Q. "At the time that you asked for this investigation, isn't it true that the people at Metropolitan didn't know one way or the other, back on November 4th, 1975, whether this was an accident or a suicide?"

A. "Well—to tell you—it does appear that— it is not definite, one way or the other."

Q. "Do you see that last paragraph there?"

A. "Yes, sir."

Q. "The date that this letter was written is before any investigation took place; isn't that correct?"

A. "Yes, sir. This was ordering an investigation."

Q. "Okay. So before any investigation took place, the claims department and Metropolitan had already formed the opinion that this appeared to be suicide— right?"

A. "Well—I guess the—I guess it could be considered that."

Q. "That's what the letter states; doesn't it?"

A. "Yes."

This was the breakthrough I had been looking for. Danz started out stating that there was no premature conclusion of suicide, but then he had to agree reluctantly that before any outside investigation was requested, the claims department at Metropolitan had decided the death was a suicide.

There was some conflict among witnesses about what happened after Retail Credit's investigative reports came back to Metropolitan. Danz ordered the investigating firm to seek additional information. At first this looked as if Metropolitan wanted to be more thorough before making up its mind. On closer examination, it appeared that the additional information being sought was merely corroborative evidence to substantiate the claim denial. For example, Metropolitan was relying upon one story which had David Frazier hallucinating in Vietnam flashbacks. We knew this was incorrect because David's army time was spent in Hawaii. He never set foot in Vietnam. I asked Danz point-blank if he had tried to find out whether David had ever been in Vietnam:

Shernoff: "You didn't want to corroborate at this point, or you didn't direct anybody to corroborate or verify at this point whether the insured was in Vietnam or not; is that correct?"

Danz: "That's true."

Q. "So the two statements you wanted to corroborate, the two that you picked out to corroborate, were two statements that would help Metropolitan deny the claim. Is that correct?"

A. "I would say yes."

Q. "Sir, assuming just for the purpose of my question David Frazier made statements such as, 'They're going to get me. They're going to get me,' when the boat neared the entrance of the Channel Islands Harbor and then when the boat got near the breakwater. Assume he suddenly ducked down and told Curtis to get down, as if he expected to be shot at. Then assume, at this point he stood up, put a hand on the safety rail, and jumped overboard.

"Would that indicate to you, one way or the other, whether it was an accident or suicide?"

Willcox objected immediately to that question, but the court overruled him. I restated the question after some argument.

Shernoff: "Those facts to you, sir, would not indicate that somebody is trying to destroy himself; would they?"

Danz: "I have to go along with that."

This hurt Metropolitan because Danz had already admitted that their investigation may have been biased from the beginning. Now he was agreeing with me that even under their version of the facts, it did not look as though David had tried to destroy himself.

Danz was getting tired on the witness stand. I could see that Willcox was upset and his colleague, Manfried Stucki, a large man with a generally calm demeanor, was fidgeting, shaking his head back and forth and shutting his eyes in frustration. Besides the Adams, Duque & Hazeltine lawyers, Metropolitan had several people from its legal department in the courtroom to observe the proceedings. They looked generally unhappy and downcast as Danz continued to testify.

I had the handwritten document blown up on a three-foot by five-foot cardboard display board. There was no mistaking what it said. I approached Danz gently. First I read the memo out loud.

"We now have additional reports which only confirm what we already know. While there is considerable opinion that he did commit suicide, I still doubt we could sustain a denial in court."

"Did you see that?"

Danz: "Yes, sir."

Q. "Who was Mr. Pfaffenbach writing that to?"

A. "Me, sir."

Q. "When he said, 'I still doubt we would sustain a denial in court,' in your mind what was he referring to by the word 'court'?"

A. "I would imagine a court of law. If I can think of what he was thinking about, sir."

Q. "Did you at this time ask him why he had those doubts?"

A. "No, sir, I don't recall asking him."

Q. "And what was his position again?"

A. "He was assistant supervisor."

Q. "How many people did he supervise?"

A. "Six, I believe."

Q. "When he wrote on the bottom of that,

'unless you want to deny now, try for a compromise later when she complains'; do you see that?''

A. "Yes, sir."

Q. "Would it be true, sir, then, that if she'd never complained at all, she would not ever be in a position to get a compromise?"

A. "Well, I will take it if there was no comeback, that she was satisfied with the situation."

Q. "If there was no comeback, the widow would be satisfied with the decision and there would be no compromise payment —is that right?"

A. "Yes, sir."

Q. "That would be the end of the matter?"

A. "Yes, sir."

Q. "Now, when you got that memo from Mr. Pfaffenbach, you just wrote on here— these are your words, 'Deny (refer any protests).'"

A. "Yes."

Q. "Is that correct."

A. "Yes, sir."

Q. "Between the time you got the memo from Mr. Pfaffenbach and you wrote the words 'Deny (refer any protests),' did you do anything other than review the file?"

A. "No, sir."

Q. "Did you talk to anybody?"

A. "No, sir, not that I recall."

This was all the ammunition I needed to make my closing argument. I was sure that I had proved beyond a shadow of doubt that Metropolitan knew the claim was payable but had tried to wriggle out of it.

In my closing argument for this phase of the trial, I had to convince the jury that the death was an accident, not suicide—and that Metropolitan's handling of the claim was in bad faith. Rather than concentrating on the evidence we brought to court, I decided to use the evidence that came right from Metropolitan's own witness and its own documents. I first reminded the jury about Danz's testimony concerning Metropolitan version of the facts:

"Let me read you the question I asked [Mr. Danz] and the answer he gave: Their version of the facts. I asked him, 'Assuming it was true David Frazier said "They're going to get me. They're going to get me." he put a hand on the safety rail, and jumped overboard.'

"I said to Danz, 'Those facts, sir, would not indicate that somebody is trying to destroy himself, would it?'

"And his answer was—Mr. Danz's answer under oath —'I have go along with that.'

"So either way, either version—he accidentally fell overboard or he suffered delusions and jumped— supports [death by] accidental means under the definition of this insurance policy and under the law. I think Metropolitan knew that, and I'll get into that when I get to their memos.

"He didn't jump overboard and say, 'I want to drown.' There was no suicide note. He was happy.

He and Mary had just bought a car the week before. He was married, had a child. No drugs. No alcohol. Pretty good solid citizen for a kid. Worked at a good job, post office. Nothing to support suicide. He went with his family fishing. If he wanted to commit suicide, why wouldn't he do it while they were 50 miles out to sea at night? Do you wait until you get back to the harbor? There just was absolutely nothing to support suicide."

I next reminded the jury of Danz's testimony concerning the letter to the outside investigating firm, Retail Credit. This would give the jury a perspective of Metropolitan's state of mind right from the start.

"This is the claim file that was produced in this case. These are the documents that were in Metropolitan Life Insurance's possession when this case was handled. This file tells what they had in front of them at the time, and it also records the notes of what they did.

"This letter was written before they did any investigation whatsoever. All they had in front of them is what Mary Frazier sent them. And now they were going to ask Retail Credit, an investigating agency, to go out and investigate, and in that letter they said, at the bottom, 'As it would appear the insured attempted suicide, we would appreciate a full report of investigation concerning any motive for suicide, et cetera.'

"They were directing them in the beginning to do what? 'Go out and get motives for suicide. We feel it's suicide. You go out and get the motives for us.'

"This is not like an independent investigation where you say to somebody, 'Hey, go out and get all the facts so we can make an intelligent decision.' No, they don't tell them that.

"They tell them: 'We think it's suicide. You go out and get us the motive so we can deny this claim.' And that's exactly what happened from day one. I'll show you exactly how it falls into place.

"When I asked Mr. Danz a question about this letter. I said: 'Okay. So before any investigation took place, the claims department and Metropolitan already formed the opinion that this appeared to be suicide, right?' "

A. " 'Well—I guess—I guess it could be considered that.' "

Q. " 'That's what the letter states, doesn't it?' "

A. " 'Yes.' "

"This is Mr. Danz. It's not me. It's not Bill Shernoff. This is Mr. Danz, their main witness, the guy that denied the claim, under oath saying before any investigation took place, they already formed the opinion it was suicide.

"Is that conscious disregard of a person's rights? It sure is. Making up your mind before you even have an investigation? It sure is.

"And then directing the investigation to try and come in the way you preconceived it. Is that fair? Is that good faith and fair dealing? That's probably the highest form of conscious disregard of a person's rights under the insurance policy one could imagine."

For good measure, I mentioned the point about how selective Mr. Danz was in corroborating certain conflicting evidence.

"Mr. Danz wants two statements corroborated, he

still didn't want to find out if David was in Vietnam or not. No. He just corroborated two statements that would help deny this claim, and that's all."

I did not know what I was going to say about those memos until I got to that point in my argument. Somehow I always have great faith that a jury will know that I really believe what I am saying when it's honest and it comes from the heart.

"Ladies and gentlemen, I think that memo speaks more loudly than anything else in this case. It says what they had on their mind, what they did, and why they did it. It certainly says more than what Mr. Willcox is going to try to tell you three or four or five or six or seven years later. That is the proof of the pudding right there.

"We were able to get their in-house memos through court process, and they tell the story. Metropolitan knew they didn't have enough reason to deny this claim. They knew they should have paid this claim, but instead of doing the fair and the right thing, they tried to deny it and hope to get away perhaps by paying nothing at all if there was no complaint. You heard Mr. Danz say that would end the matter. And if there was a complaint, if the poor lady complained, 'we'd pay her less, try to compromise it.'

"Now, if that's the way to do insurance business in this country, God help us on our insurance claims. This is conscious disregard of a person's rights in the highest form, and luckily we have their own memos to prove it.

"Just put that memo against the letter that they sent out when they denied the claim. Here is what is going on at One Madison Avenue. Here is what is going on behind closed walls. Here is what are the real thoughts, and here is what goes to Mary Frazier, in L.A., a letter that says, in fact, 'We have made a most thorough investigation in this matter.' They made an investigation in this matter directed only towards proving their preconceived notion that there was a suicide and that's it.

"They tell Mary Frazier that [investigation shows] under the circumstances death was due to self-destruction. That's what they tell her, but they say in their own memos, 'We don't have enough to sustain a denial in court.'

"Ladies and gentlemen, I think you know what this case is about. It is really not about drowning or negligence or anything of the sort. It's about whether an insurance company treated a claimant fairly in good faith or was guilty of conscious disregard of her rights."

The jury came back with the following special findings: they found the death accidental, they found Metropolitan's claims handling was in bad faith, and they found that Metropolitan's claims handling amounted to malice. The malice finding was important because it would allow us to put on evidence of Metropolitan's financial worth and to argue for punitive damages.

The second phase of the trial went quickly. We put Mary Frazier on the witness stand to testify about the mental distress she suffered when Metropolitan told her that her husband killed himself and how her emotions turned to anger.

We then put into evidence Metropolitan's financial report. We showed that Metropolitan's income in 1981 was $371 million, or just slightly over $1 million per day. This was after all expenses, dividends, and taxes were paid. We also put into evidence Metropolitan's net worth (they call it surplus) which was an astounding $2,354,000,000. The company was making over $1 million per day and had a staggering net worth.

What would a reasonable punishment be? I asked myself that question and spent a considerable amount of time discussing it in front of the jury. It boiled down to this: I asked the jury to punish Metropolitan Life approximately one or two weeks' worth of earnings. This was somewhere between $7 million and $12 million.

Metropolitan's lawyer, James Willcox, made an argument which I thought was somewhat strange. In essence, he claimed that being caught was punishment enough. He put it this way:

> "You are not required to have a finding of punitive damages, and I ask you to consider and think to yourself—I don't know how recently any of you have been stopped by a policeman or even gotten a parking ticket, but something where you've been fined. Sure, it hurts to pay the fine. It also hurts just to get the ticket. Not just to be caught, but be found to have done something wrong to which you are subject to a fine, to punishment. Even failing to return an overdue library book. I think we all get mad at ourselves.

> " 'How can I be so stupid as to not have returned the book?' It isn't the fifty cents you have to pay the library; it's the upset that you didn't do what you should have done.

> "Now, counsel has made a very big deal out of the numbers. I told you in opening statement on this aspect of the case that the numbers are going to be big, because Metropolitan is a very large company. They've been doing business for a long, long time, longer than any of us have been alive, and it's grown.

> "Look at the actual facts. Look at the actual figures.

What would be fair, if in fact you decided any punishment is merited whatsoever. What is an appropriate fine if you were the judge here and saying that this defendant ought to be fined?

"It isn't enough that they've been brought into court and gone through a proceeding and been told that they acted wrongfully, been told that they acted with malice and have been assessed and ordered to pay actual compensatory damages to the plaintiff. You are the judges saying, 'No, that's not enough. We have to fine this defendant because what has already happened isn't enough.' That's what you have to consider."

The last words in the closing argument were my rebuttal. I just could not stand still for Willcox's argument that Metropolitan should come out of this case with little or no punitive damages.

"Ladies and gentlemen, I'm going to be fairly short in this part, but what I hear Mr. Willcox saying is: 'It's okay. We are in a court of law. We were found guilty of bad faith and malice. Don't punish us.'

"That would be nice, I suppose. He talks about a parking ticket. A parking ticket is one thing. People can have momentary lapses, but the jury instruction on malice was conscious disregard of rights and safety. I think everybody knows that in any sort of a traffic situation if a court of law finds you having been guilty of malice in your conduct, consciously disregarding rights of others, you're lucky if you get away with punishment of one week's earnings.

"There has to be meaning to the law. To find malice but find no punishment, [no] bad faith, no punishment, is a joke. There is no meaning to the finding.

"The law has to have significance. The law has to live. The law lives through people like you.

"Let's respect the law. Let's give meaning to the law. Let's not say, 'We find malice and go on your way, Metropolitan.' The law should have the same meaning for everybody, rich or poor. Rich or poor should be treated alike."

The jury retired for deliberation Friday morning at 9:40 A.M., March 11, and continued most of the day. Their deliberations were broken by a weekend recess and were resumed Monday morning. After lunch there was a gathering of lawyers, witnesses, and observers outside the courtroom. At about 1:30 P.M., we all saw Judge Bigelow slip into the judge's entrance of the courtroom, and a few minutes later we were called. The jury had a verdict.

"Ladies and gentlemen of the jury," Judge Bigelow began, "have you arrived at a verdict?"

"Yes, Your Honor," the foreman responded.

It took a moment or two to get past the technicalities. We were all waiting for the amounts of damages. He then said, matter-of-factly:

Accidental death benefit: $12,000

Emotional distress: $150,000

Punitive damages: $8,000,000

This was the largest punitive-damage award I had ever heard a jury come back with in a double-indemnity insurance bad faith case. A widow, a poor black woman from Watts, had toppled one of America's corporate giants with an $8 million punishment over a $12,000 claim. I believe it was justified, and I hope it will convince insurance companies that they'd better shape up or suffer similar consequences.

When the jury foreman read the amount, most people thought they hadn't heard correctly. Several reporters appeared magically and the *Los Angeles Times* had a

photographer on the scene posthaste. The next day Mary
Frazier, a quiet woman, a dental technician who wore her
white uniform to court, appeared on the front page of the
*Times.* I was standing behind her, and above us the headline
read: "Widow Awarded $8 Million." The kicker followed
with "Sued Insurer for Not Paying $12,000 Claim."

When it came time to argue the motion for new trial,
Metropolitan tried to convince the judge that the verdict
should not stand at all. Judge Bigelow denied the motion,
but reduced the punitive-damage award to $2 million.

I thought that Metropolitan should have been happy with
that development and would pay. Instead, the company
appealed, even after the judge's reduction. The primary
point raised in the appeal did not concern the merits of the
case, but rather addressed a technicality: the statute of
limitations. This is a law which mandates that lawsuits must
be filed within a certain period of time. If the lawsuit is not
filed within that period of time, it is lost forever, regardless
of how meritorious the case may be. Since the law of "bad
faith" is a new legal doctrine, the question of the proper
statute of limitations has not yet been resolved firmly. Mary
Frazier's lawsuit was filed slightly over two years from the
time her claim was denied. She did not realize that she had a
lawsuit for quite some time because she believed the letter
she got from Metropolitan which stated it had made a
thorough investigation and had concluded that her
husband died by virtue of suicide. It was not until the trial
of her first lawsuit against the charter boat company that
she realized that her husband's death was probably not due
to suicide.

The decision of the District Court of Appeal contained
good news and bad news. The good news was that it held
the jury was justified in finding Metropolitan's conduct to
be in bad faith and that the bad faith was clearly established
by Metropolitan's own records.

It also found sufficient evidence in the record to support a verdict for damages for emotional distress. The decision held that such damages were not barred by the statute of limitations which the District Court of Appeal concluded was four years.

Then came the bad news. The District Court of Appeal differentiated between compensatory damages and punitive damages for the purpose of the statute of limitations. It held that the statute of limitations was only two years for the punitive damages. This meant that the punitive damages would be stricken from the judgment and only the damages due under the insurance policy and for emotional distress could be recovered in this case.

This case stands out as one of the best examples of why it may be important to question a "Payment Refused" letter from an insurance company, even if it sounds quite official. In this case, the jury found that what Mary Frazier was told by Metropolitan concerning the death of her husband was not true. The jury found that his death was not due to suicide, but due to accidental means and that the claim should have been paid.

This case shows why it is so important to act as soon as you can if you feel you have suffered damages as a result of some wrongdoing. As you can see, sleeping on your rights for too long a period of time can be costly.

# Chapter 9

# They Even Give the Business to Business

Insurance companies don't confine bad faith practices only to individuals, they also give the business to business. In recent years, the insurance industry has been pulling the same stunts against the big boys as it has against the little guy. Significantly, businesses are now starting to sue their insurance carriers for bad faith. Just a few years ago, all insurance bad faith cases were fought on behalf of individual policyholders. Now 10 percent of my caseload stems from bad faith suits initiated by businesses. Not only is this trend healthy, it reveals that more and more American businesses, small and large, support bad faith litigation as a necessary remedy against unfair insurance practices.

"At the moment, I can't see any other way of getting at the problem," comments Keith A. Cunningham, chief executive officer of United Nuclear Corporation. Cunningham maintains that punitive-damage awards are a result of abusive insurance behavior. U.N.C. recently won over $50 million damages (including $25 million in punitive damages) from Allendale Mutual Insurance Company. A New Mexico district court ruled that Allendale Mutual acted in bad faith in denying U.N.C. payments when a dam holding uranium waste collapsed. Like other United States businesses, U.N.C. suffered through years of major losses and attorney fees before the court ruled against Allendale Mutual's ambiguous business-interruption policy. "It has become more advantageous for an insurance company to refuse to pay, incur attorneys' fees, and invest the money—than it is to settle up," concludes Cunningham.

One of the biggest bad faith lawsuits ever filed occurred when MGM Grand Hotel sued a multitude of insurers and its insurance broker after the insurance carriers refused to reimburse the hotel for claims settled as a result of the disastrous 1980 Las Vegas fire.

Following the tragedy, MGM discovered that it was inadequately insured and—as it is possible to do—MGM purchased a large retroactive policy. Insurance companies were willing to sell retroactive coverage because, although it was certain the loss had occurred, the extent of the loss and the length of time for payout were still unknown and the insurance companies could earn investment income on the premium until those two factors were resolved. The premium amounted to almost $40 million—an astonishing sum.

MGM Grand Hotel settled all the claims arising out of the 84 deaths and approximately 1,500 injury claims. The insurance carriers refused to reimburse MGM, claiming, among other things, that MGM paid too much money and settled the claims at too high amounts, even though a federal court found the settlements were reasonable and approved the $69 million payout. When the retroactive carriers refused to pay, MGM filed a bad faith case against them asking for massive punitive and compensatory damages.

I became associated with MGM's regular counsel, the Los Angeles law firm of Wyman, Bautzer, Rothman, Kuchel & Silbert to be the trial attorney for the case. Allen Goldman and Patty Glaser, along with many Wyman, Bautzer lawyers, had been working on the case for a couple of years. Both are brilliant lawyers and tireless workers. Allen was the chief architect of this massive piece of litigation, and Patty was assigned to be my co-counsel at the trial. There were so many lawyers representing the various insurance companies on the other side of this case that no courtroom in Las Vegas was large enough to accommodate the trial. Judge Paul Goldman quickly found a solution to this problem. He ordered the various parties to pay $125,000 into a special fund so that a courtroom could be constructed in the Las Vegas Sports Arena, which would then be large enough to hold the trial.

Then the scene was set for one of the largest trials ever to take place in America, from the standpoint of the number of lawyers and parties involved. Because of the size and complexity of the case, Judge Goldman was obliged to keep things in line with some strict rulings. For example, just prior to the start of the trial, he fined an insurance company $3,000 for bringing what he considered to be, a frivolous motion. He also fined several other insurance companies $2,000 simply for joining in that motion. He really got tough a few days prior to jury selection, when he fined another party $25,000 for not properly marking and identifying the voluminous documents to be used during the trial. I think it was his strict handling of the matter that created the climate for settlement.

As I started to select jury members, the attitude of the insurance companies began to soften when they offered a substantial settlement to avoid a full-blown trial. Then, right after the jury was selected, a settlement was reached. MGM Grand was to be paid $76 million dollars in addition to the $11 million previous paid, for a total of $87 million. The settlement itself was quite an occasion. There was a big signing ceremony, after which the judge brought in a band for a celebration. The local *Las Vegas Sun* reported this way:

### MGM Megatrial Settled
### in Festive Mood

The MGM Grand Hotel insurance megatrial ended Wednesday at the Thomas and Mack Center in a festive mood, as District Judge Paul Goldman approved the $87.5 million out-of-court settlement.

Champagne, rock music and laughter filled the special courtroom at the center after the judge adjourned the proceedings, having just received a T-shirt inscribed in Latin with 'You can never have too much insurance' from all the lawyers on the case.

Goldman also had all the lawyers sign a large color poster of Howard Hughes' flying boat, the *Spruce Goose*, an unwieldly and oversized aircraft to which Goldman has compared the megatrial setup.

...In the settlement, MGM will receive $87.5 million for nonpayment of retroactive insurance, believed to be the largest settlement in an insurance case ever. It will receive the money from Las Vegas insurance broker Frank B. Hall, Del Webb Corp. and 28 carriers for companies that sold retroactive insurance to MGM in the wake of the Nov. 21, 1980, fire that took eighty-four lives and hospitalized 400.

...More than one person remarked that the trial's end reminded them of the last day of school.

Bailiff Del La Fountain, in asking lawyers not to take the signs hanging from the ceiling identifying them, couldn't contain himself.

..."Don't take the signs," he said. "You people from insurance companies are lucky to be getting out of here with your suits."

Settlements happen quite often, and it is not unusual for cases to be settled "on the courthouse steps." Indeed, over 90 percent of these cases actually involve out-of-court settlements just before a trial is to begin. The jurors may feel cheated that they did not get to hear and decide the case. However, their service is invaluable. If it were not for the jury sitting there, ready to make the decision, chances are that cases would never be settled. Obviously, it is to the financial advantage of the insurance carrier to hold onto the money until the last possible moment. By virtue of the fact that a jury is ready and willing to hear the case, even though the case sometimes never gets to them, makes the system work.

Confronted with unfair insurance practices, small businesses are also seeking relief in the courts. Not long ago, the former Source Commodities Corporation in New York City sued Aetna Casualty and Surety Company because the carrier refused to pay the small brokerage house for losses caused by an employee's alleged dishonesty. Source Commodities carried a policy known as a stockbroker's blanket bond, designed to cover the exact kind of loss incurred by the brokerage firm. A key document in the case was an Aetna interoffice memo which evaluated the claim and concluded that the carrier had no chance of gaining a favorable decision in court. A jury awarded Source Commodities $100,000 in compensatory damages and $200,000 in punitive damages. The New York lawyer who handled that case has informed me that the case has been settled.

When William Burke bought a swimming pool company franchise in the 1950s, he purchased comprehensive liability insurance with the National Union Fire Insurance Company of Pittsburgh. Eighteen years later, Burke's company was sued by a boy who dove backward off a diving board and hit his head on an underwater love seat. The boy was paralyzed. The suit claimed that the swimming pool's design was faulty. When Burke turned the matter over to National Union, the company refused to pay. First it claimed there was no policy in existence. When the policy turned up, National Union then claimed there was no coverage. A jury disagreed and found bad faith, and awarded Burke and his company the $13 million in punitive damages, plus $659,231 in compensatory damages. The case is now on appeal.

The law of insurance bad faith is coming to the rescue of

almost everyone who feels he or she has a grievance. Even the Republican Central Committee of San Diego County has filed a bad faith lawsuit. They retained our San Diego office of Shernoff & Levine in a lawsuit demanding punitive damages and attorney fees against Fireman's Fund Insurance Company. The Central Committee was forced to provide its own defense after Wanda Smith Vail, owner of the *Independent Republican* newspaper, sued the Central Committee in 1980 over a complex business issue. Like most comprehensive liability policies, the Central Committee's policy showed that the insurance company was obliged to defend the insured against any alleged property damage or bodily injury caused by particular occurrences—whether or not the allegations were groundless, false or fraudulent. Fireman's Fund Insurance Company refused to provide a defense, forcing the Central Committee to go to the expense of defending itself. The case was settled during the middle of the trial. It was a whopping settlement resulting in a huge sum of money being transferred from Fireman's Fund to the Republicans' coffers.

Fire insurance claims have become fertile grounds for bad faith cases. Fire insurance carriers seem to have a penchant for heaping insult upon injury when their cries of arson are nearly as loud as the fire sirens. Nobody denies that arson is a problem, but what happens when the accusations are made without adequate investigation? When a fire insurance carrier cries foul play and blames "suspicious origin" as a reason to deny payments, it may be using just one of the many pieces of ammunition it keeps in its arsenal of delays.

Delaying tactics, including arson accusations, disputed fine-print clauses and discrepancies in appraised valuations make fire victims vulnerable to severe losses and even bankruptcy. Fire insurers know this, and they know that fears of total loss and ruin frequently influence small businesses to settle claims for amounts much below actual losses.

Arson accusations are the most feared of insurance carriers' delaying tactics because victims not only suffer financial losses from the fire, but are then subjected to public humiliation when their supposed protectors accuse them of high crime. It's the sort of thing the media capitalizes on, and I know of instances when innocent fire victims left town because of the bad publicity. It's hard to imagine a more bleak turn of events than to have your house or business burn down and then have your fire insurer unfairly zap you with charges of arson.

"It was a nightmare and it continues," says Vic Perry, one of two businessmen who were accused of burning down their small auto-parts store. On a cold February night in 1977, the store blew up, destroying the business. The men sought benefits under their Royal Globe Insurance Company fire policy and were refused payment. The insurance company filed a lawsuit demanding that the county government relieve them of any financial responsibility due to the fire.

"When that happened, it hit the media—and we were guilty before any trial took place," says Perry. "If it was just fighting over money, that would have been one thing. But they assassinate your character. They are out to do you in, and they have all the professionals and money to do it. It is like a death in the family. You never get over it," adds Perry.

Although the businessmen were never questioned by the police or the fire department—or prosecuted by the district attorney—the insurance company stuck arrogantly by the charge that the two businessmen had committed arson. Six years later, after all investigations were concluded and no arrests had been made, Royal Globe continued to insinuate arson during the trial.

David Lipsky, one of my former partners, won a large jury award for Quinton Sondergaard and Victor Perry, owners of

Economy Motors in Bishop, California—but not until after the two businessmen and their families were forced to leave the small town of Bishop. Lipsky proved that the explosion was accidental, the result of a faulty butane heater. After the jury verdict covering that part of the trial ended, the way was open for bad faith and punitive damages.

The case was eventually settled for over $750,000. But the emotional damages that go beyond money remain. Perry, who now lives in northern California, suffered a stroke recently. His doctors attribute the ailment to the stress Perry has lived under since the fire. The experience has caused Perry to be bitter. "If insurance companies were truthful at one time, they aren't today. I am firmly convinced now that they are out to deny your claim or pay as little as possible, even before the smoke goes away," he says. Lipsky calls this case a "typical fire case. The insurance company doesn't do an adequate investigation, and then it decides it doesn't want to pay you so it accuses you of fraud. It happens a lot."

Disputes in business insurance cases are complicated and varied. Insurance companies have hundreds of methods of calculating losses, many of which are bound to cause disputes and therefore delay in payment. For example, how do you calculate losses for business interruption? Different accounting methods will yield different results, and an insurer can play around with figures deliberately for months and even years.

Property damage is disputed similarly. An insurance company with all its resources has no problem whatsoever in throwing up roadblocks over value. The insurance carrier always demands receipts for destroyed or stolen items, but neither individuals nor businesses keep receipts for every single inventory item. Sometimes receipts are destroyed by the fire. The insurer may insist that until the value of each and every item is established by receipts, it has no obligation to pay anything.

In other cases, when replacement cost is the measure of recovery, insurers will invite contractors to make bids. These estimates, of course, can vary greatly. A favorite tactic is for an insurance company to obtain bids from contractors whose primary business involves repairing damaged property following an insured's loss. The livelihood of these contractors depends on the goodwill of the insurance company. The insurer may induce the contractor to submit an unrealistically low bid and then offer that amount as settlement of the claim.

Another frequently used technique for denying claims is to foist off responsibility on another insurance carrier. Insurers have ways of claiming that the losses occurred when the victim was insured by another company. Thus, claiming no liability, or that its coverage is "secondary" and another carrier "primary," relieves it of liability until the primary carrier has paid. When several carriers are involved, as is frequently the situation in business cases, the finger pointing looks like a pretzel. I've seen cases when insurers have tried to set the loss on another insurer who hadn't carried the victim's coverage for years.

Then there is the most loved clause of the insurance industry—the "act of God" exclusion. Claims adjusters turn evangelical at the drop of a hat, blaming all things on God when it suits them. Despite the fact that He may have caused the floods, landslides, storms, and blizzards, the insurer is nevertheless often liable for the damage. Don't be fooled! In a given disaster, the contractor may be just as responsible as the Deity in many cases, but the contractor's negligence is what the insurance company has to pay for.

Many businesses, large and small, do not pay enough attention to their insurance coverage. They often invest more time and money on a Christmas party than on investigating their carriers and reading their policies. No wonder they are surprised when the insurance carrier is not on the scene immediately, a pen in one hand, a check in the other. However, insurance carriers often take advantage of policyholder ignorance. There is no excuse for shoddy insurance practices, and the insured should not be punished for not knowing as much as he might have.

The insurance industry has lulled us into thinking that each agent is a messenger of protection, an Olympic torchbearer, a savior from ultimate devastation. Insurance advertising on television and in the press shows the claims adjuster on the scene even before the ashes have cooled. Insurers have created an expectation that claims will be paid promptly and fairly. That is a reasonable expectation. Unfortunately, it has to be enforced by the courts and the people who serve on juries.

# Chapter 10

# Banks Beware, You're Next

Is it possible to apply the same principles of ordinary justice, which are required of your insurance company to your bank's shenanigans? Although the "good faith and fair dealing" requirements have applied to insurance companies since the day Michael Egan made legal history, the same legal principles are creeping into other areas of the law where large business has a special or fiduciary relationship with its customers. Banks are a good example.

When Jack Pitzer first came to my office in Claremont, California, I was somewhat surprised. The Pitzers are well-known pioneers in Claremont, part of the establishment. I could not imagine why they would have an unresolved gripe against Security Pacific National Bank. First Jack explained that he thought most lawyers would not sue banks because of the mutually beneficial relationship that banks enjoy with attorneys because of probate, corporate, and other legal matters.

He had heard of the obligations of good faith and fair dealing an insurance company owes its policyholders, and he thought banks should also be required to deal as fairly in trust matters. Jack had also heard about our office and felt we were the ones to take on Security Pacific for what he considered its blatant breach of good faith in handling a rather large trust that was set up by his father's will.

Clifford Pitzer set up the trust with Security Pacific Bank for the benefit of Jack, his sister, Pat Lautmann, and his widow, Fern Pitzer. Mrs. Pitzer was to receive the income of

the trust for as long as she lived. In accepting the trustee-
ship, Security Pacific was obligated by law to manage the
trust, including its citrus groves, for the benefit of Fern
Pitzer. This really shouldn't have been a large problem, as
Clifford Pitzer had managed the acres as active and successful citrus groves for many years, with the help of his son
Jack and a foreman. When Clifford died, Mrs. Pitzer, with
the help of Jack and the foreman, managed the groves.

I had been so busy with my bad faith actions against
insurance companies that handling similar suits against
banks had never occurred to me. If an insurance company
must treat its policyholders fairly and in good faith,
certainly a bank should also be required to do so when
handling a trust for beneficiaries. The law would be very
similar—or if it wasn't it should be—and I decided to accept
the challenge.

Jack's gripe was simple. The Pitzer family trust was worth
about $500,000. It included 20 acres of citrus groves that
had been operated by the Pitzer family for years. These
groves provided Mrs. Pitzer an income of approximately
$1,000 per month. Suddenly, without the Pitzers'
knowledge or consent, the bank sold this land to a
developer for a price the Pitzers claimed was far below
market value. To add insult to injury, the bank simply gave
away various items of personal property that were
necessary to run a grove: wind machines, smudge pots,
sprinkler systems, a flatbed truck, and some revolving
funds.

What really steamed Jack Pitzer was what the bank did
with the well. This is what made him angry enough to come
to my office. Jack owned and operated the grove next to
the grove held by the Pitzer family trust. The source of
water for Jack's grove was a well located on the trust
property. Jack had an agreement with his father that he
could use this well and had been doing so for over twenty
years. When the bank sold the land, the well was destroyed

and Jack's water supply was cut off. Cutting off someone's water in California is serious business. That the land was sold to a developer who had no use for the well and who immediately made plans for subdividing the groves made the whole transaction even more unsavory.

Mrs. Pitzer was a sweet elderly woman who hated the thought of litigation. Eventually, even she became so angry at the bank's behavior that she agreed reluctantly to go along with Jack's recommendation to sue the bank. When Security Pacific took over as trustee in 1974, an evaluation of the property was made so that the bank could set its trustee fees. The land was evaluated by bank-appointed appraisers in July of that year at $368,000, or approximately $18,000 per acre.

Four months later, Mrs. Pitzer decided to sell the family residence situated next to the grove property. Her decision, however, became mired in complications. Part of the residence property had been deeded mistakenly to the trust. Mrs. Pitzer had to purchase 6,000 square feet of the trust property so the new owner could take the deed to the titled portion of the residence property.

Security Pacific charged Mrs. Pitzer $3,500 to purchase this 6,000-square-foot portion of the land. That price was the equivalent of $25,000 per acre, and the Pitzers had complained to the bank at that time, without success.

Subsequently, Jack told bank officials about the lost water rights. He explained that the various items on the property were valuable and should have been sold, not given away. He also insisted that the land was worth more than the developer was paying. The bank did nothing.

According to the bank, the groves were losing money and the trust could no longer afford to pay Mrs. Pitzer her monthly allowance. Using this as an excuse, Security Pacific sold the groves. When the Pitzers complained, bank officials met with Fern Pitzer and tried to "explain" things to her.

Fern later testified at the trial that she felt all they were trying to do was "mollify an old lady." The bank had told her that the land had been exposed properly to the real estate market before the actual sale took place; that the price was good value for the land and the items that went with it; that the bank had not realized before the sale that Jack had been using the well to irrigate his own groves; and that if she wanted to purchase the well back, that the trust would have to pay for it.

As soon as the lawsuit was filed, we were hit with an unusual pretrial defense: the bank asserted that this was strictly a probate matter and that any transgression in a trust of this kind is immune from punitive damages. Security Pacific claimed that any violations of its trust duties could result only in the imposition of surcharges by the probate judge. These generally amounted to very small slaps on the wrist. We knew right away that we had to do some fancy research.

I assigned Lou Fazzi, a young attorney in our office, to assist me on this case. He worked in the library for several days and concluded that a punitive-damage suit for breach of trust was possible, even though this was also a probate matter. The bank made several motions to knock our punitive-damage lawsuit out of court at the outset, but each time we were able to convince the court that probate should not be a shield for fraudulent or malicious behavior, and that a civil lawsuit for punitive damages could take place, side-by-side, with a probate matter. There did not seem to be any direct precedent on this legal point, which made the case even more significant in our eyes. It was important to do the groundwork.

The trial would last twenty-four days over a three-month period and produce about 2,500 pages of transcript. As usual, I asked the Pitzers to be my first witnesses. As they testified, certain details began to fall in place. But the witnesses from Security Pacific were probably the most critical in the whole lawsuit.

Jack told how he unexpectedly learned of the sale. In mid-February, Jack happened to see Roger Wheeler, a well-known local realtor. Wheeler told him that the family grove property was for sale. Jack immediately called a bank officer to ask about his water rights. He spoke to Francis Curran, then an assistant vice-president in the real estate division of the bank. Curran assured him he would get back to him before the property was sold. No one called Jack.

Again, Jack Pitzer learned of the transactions from people he saw on the property who told him they were buying the land. Jack again called Curran, who this time around told him the matter was none of his business. After the Pitzers' testimony, as witnesses from the bank were brought in to testify, the full story emerged.

When the decision was made to ready the property for sale, evidence showed that through October 1975 the appraised value of the groves and the extras was approximately $362,000, with a list price of $410,000. In November the bank seemed to have second thoughts about the price of the land. Officials from Security Pacific consulted with Claremont realtor Roger Wheeler, a man whose expertise in turning over groves to developers was well known and whose landholdings in the same general area were considerable.

Following that meeting, a new appraisal was announced and the results constituted one of the more remarkable events in the history of postwar Southern California real estate. The land was devalued by about half, and the appraised value dropped to $241,000 with a suggested list price of $252,000. The bank's highest-ranking officials held a meeting to approve the sale price of this real estate property—entrusted by Clifford Pitzer to protect his widow and children—at a price $125,000 lower than previous recent appraisals. This lower price was approved even though the bank had based its trustee fees on the higher value all along. The bank officials professed that they had no minutes of the meeting.

I was able to make a lot out of this curious turn of events—this drastic reduction in price which no one could document, and for which nobody was responsible. The bank's own appraisals showed the value of the groves dropping from a suggested list price of $410,000 to $252,000. There appeared to be no apparent rhyme or reason for this historic drop in the value of raw land—especially a large section of unincorporated county land that was due to be annexed to the city of Claremont.

Just west of that land, on property already annexed, subdivision housing was going up with unprecedented speed. The housing boom in the Claremont foothills had begun, and Roger Wheeler had been selling land—including his own—to developers for construction. This profitable land development included some old groves just west of the Pitzer property, so there was no way to conclude that raw land in that area was going to lose value. Had Security Pacific held on to that trust property a year or two longer, the value of the trust would have increased dramatically.

In January 1976, the property was listed by realtors Wheeler, Steffen, Garrison. The price totaled $270,000, which included the sundry items, at a value of $29,000; the land was being sold for $241,000. The Pitzers were not informed of the decision to sell.

The property was sold on March 3, 1976, to Edward Bell, the first person who made an offer. The purchase price totaled $240,000, period. Bell intended to subdivide the land. He had no use for the well or any of the sundry items that were supposed to sell for $29,000. It appeared that the bank simply gave Bell these items. Bell destroyed the well since he had no use for it.

We showed that the property was sold to the first buyer who came along, and that Bell, within a few months, resold part of the land at a $22,000 profit; that the bank had made no effort to sell the sundry items separately; that there was a strong circumstantial case for the bank's actually being aware of Jack's use of the well to irrigate his own groves; and that mere logic dictated that if the bank had wrongfully given away the well, the Pitzer trust should not have to buy it back.

And that was just the beginning. The trial itself focused strongly on Security Pacific's conduct regarding the very profitable loans it made subsequently on the property, *one of which was actually negotiated and completed while the bank was still trustee.*

A few months after the developer, Bell, sold the northern 10 acres, he sold the south 10-acre parcel for $192,000, making an even greater profit than he had on the northern acreage. The south 10 acres were brought by Parkland Development Co., the principals of which were two old and good customers of Security Pacific Bank. The bank loaned Parklane the money to help buy the land and then, a few months later, granted the company a $1,915,000 construction loan. Trial testimony showed that the bank had contemplated making both loans during the period that it was still trustee of the Pitzer property. Furthermore, it also showed that Parklane was planning to repay the purchase loan out of the construction-loan funds.

Security Pacific officials suffered from serious lapses of memory. They gave the appearance of being arrogant, and when they could not come up with decent explanations for their conduct, they simply gave incredible excuses.

One striking example was the testimony of John Sohmer, a twenty-year bank employee and the trust administrator at the time of the trial. I asked him about a handwritten memo from the bank's files, a memo that had already been introduced into evidence. It indicated a telephone call between Sohmer and Jack Pitzer:

> Q. "Do you remember the contents of the phone call?"

A. "Not specifically, no."

Q. "As a matter of fact, it is true, is it not, that you don't have a recollection of that phone call other than what's on that piece of paper?"

A. "No, I remember Mr. Pitzer calling."

A. "But you don't recall the contents of the phone call?"

A. "No, I do not."

Q. "So, when you testified just a minute ago on direct examination that you remembered that he did not mention any inquiry about his water rights, you didn't really remember that, either, did you?"

A. "I remembered only what I told the gentleman in this memo."

Q. "But you just indicated here to the jury that you didn't really specifically recall the contents of that phone call; isn't that correct?"

A. "That's correct."

Q. "So you don't know one way or the other from your own memory whether Mr. Pitzer mentioned anything about the use of the water from the well; isn't that correct?"

A. "I don't remember him mentioning it."

Q. "One way or the other?"

A. "Correct."

Q. "But you testified in response to your

> lawyer's question that he didn't mention anything about the use of the water; didn't you?"

A. "To my recollection."

Q. "You don't have any recollection."

A. "I don't remember."

Q. "How could you say that he didn't inquire about the use of his water as he testified, if the truth is, you don't remember?"

Among the most flagrant abuses of candor during the trial was Sohmer's seeming inability to understand the concept of wholesaling, a word used by the bank officials in one of their meetings to discuss disposal of the property. We claimed from documentary evidence that as early as January 1975, bank officials had met to discuss the idea of marketing the groves—"wholesale."

Shernoff: "Now, sir, with regard to the sale of the property that you testified you were involved in, you recognize it's your duty if you are going to sell trust property to get the highest and best price you can for the beneficiaries, don't you?"

Sohmer: "Yes, I do."

Q. "That would go to any trust property, including real estate property or land. Isn't that correct?"

A. "That's correct."

Q. "Would that also mean that, like anybody else shopping around for best prices, et cetera, that you would test the market and try to get the highest and best price?"

A. "It would not be up to me as an individual to do this."

Q. "I mean the bank as the trustee, would that be one of their jobs?"

A. "Yes."

Q. "Now, with reference to one of these documents that Mr. Faith [the defense lawyer] showed you, and which is in evidence, you said there was something in that memo about selling the property to a developer, did you not?"

A. "Yes, I did."

Q. "The actual reference in that memo is not to *selling* property to a developer, is it?"

A. "Wholesaling."

Q. "Wholesaling it to a developer, that's what he says. Isn't that right?"

A. "That's correct."

Q. "Do you know what 'wholesaling' means?"

A. "No, I don't."

Q. "Have you ever bought anything at wholesale?"

A. "Not that I know of."

Q. "You've been a trust administrator for how long?"

A. "Since 1968."

Q. "And you've never heard of the word

'wholesaling'? Is that what you are trying to tell us?''

A. "Well—not during my job as a trust administrator."

Q. "I'm just asking you as an individual, what does 'wholesaling' mean?"

A. "Possibly a way to get it cheaper."

"Wholesaling" the property was, of course, a central issue in the case because the bank never gave a satisfactory explanation of why the property lost value so quickly.

The momentum just kept building and it was soon obvious that the bank officials were trying to pull the wool over everyone's eyes, including the jury's. I could feel that the jury was with me when I made the following plea:

"The problem that we are having today is that power breeds arrogance, and when you are arrogant, you start to disregard the truth and think you can get away with everything; you can do anything you want; you can cheat; you can lie; you can steal.

"Believe me, if common people did what this bank did in this case, they would go to jail. I don't care how you cut it; or how sophisticated you want to get, the bank just took the money.

"They tell her, this nice old lady who is the income beneficiary; who wouldn't hurt a fly, sitting there with all these bank officials, I can just picture it, they tell her,...[and it is right in their own lousy records], 'We had negotiated until we felt the best and highest offer had been attained.' They had negotiated? What an outright, phony, lousy lie. Who did they negotiate with? It sounds like they were telling her, 'We've been in there. We got offers. We have been negotiating; we finally got you the highest price, Mrs. Pitzer. Keep quiet. You are an old lady; sit in the corner; shut up.' "

I made as much as I could of the trust administrator's remark concerning the word "wholesaling" in the memo and the fact that he did not know what "wholesaling" meant. I took much more liberty in my closing argument than I usually do, and I probably got carried away:

"I asked him, Mr. Sohmer, what does the term 'wholesaling' mean? And can you believe it? That man sat there on the witness stand, under oath, and told this jury—and I don't know if they think we are all dumb or maybe I am losing my mind, I don't know which. He told this jury that, 'I don't know what the term "wholesaling" means.'

"They've got to think we are the biggest fools to ever come down the pike. Never heard of the term. Never bought anything at wholesale, under oath.

"Finally—finally, when I kept at him he blurted out, 'Oh, yeah,'—he had this light bulb go off in his head —'it means you get it cheaper.'

"Now, ladies and gentlemen, I think this was a telltale point in this case, because it really says what they did. They wholesaled this property, and the testimony is clear that when they sold it they made money on the loan."

By the time I got to the end of my closing argument, I had really put myself into this case, lock, stock, and barrel. I felt even more indignant about the injustice of what had happened here than in many of my insurance cases. The jury was listening intently as I finished my closing remarks:

"Concealment, misrepresentation, deception, evasion, call it what you want. If that is truth and honesty; if that is the way banks should do business in this state, that's up to you. This case is all about truth and honesty, and how people should do business, because if you find the bank's actions unconscionable, if you find a conscious disregard of people's rights, you have the power to do something about it in this case, and that is what this case is all about."

The lawyer representing the bank was J. Randall Faith. He was competent and low-key. He could not do much with the testimony about "wholesaling," other than to point out that the memo was actually written by someone else, not by Sohmer. This didn't appear to be a very effective defense. As for the outrage felt by the three beneficiaries, Faith made an argument that may have made the jury even more angry than they already were after hearing all these sordid details. He told the jury in his closing arguments:

> "The beneficiaries complained, they testified in court that they were upset because they didn't know what was going on, they weren't consulted. They learned things after the fact. Well, those are complaints that shouldn't be directed to Security Pacific....There is no evidence before you that Mr. Pitzer in his will asked that any of the three beneficiaries that are before you now have any right to manage the property, any right to be consulted about any of the sales, any right to veto any of the sales. The complaints the beneficiaries have should have been directed to Mr. Pitzer at the time he drafted his will because those were his choices."

The jury came back with an impressive punitive damage award of $3 million. $1 million each to Fern, Jack and Pat. They also awarded emotional distress damages to the three beneficiaries.

The verdict caused a terrific stink in the banking

community. Security Pacific was stunned. They were probably counting on the trial judge, Francis Garvey, who was about to retire, to help them out on posttrial motions by setting aside the verdict or at least reducing it. However, the trial judge denied the bank's motion for a new trial and let the punitive damage award stand.

Security Pacific filed the usual appeal, but before the case could wind its way all the way through the appellate process, the bank made a settlement offer and the Pitzer family, tired of the long legal treadmill, accepted it.

\* \* \*

The next bank case I became involved in was *Louis Marches* v. *Crocker National Bank*. The Marches case was referred to me by a Beverly Hills lawyer with the surprisingly similar name of Stan Chernoff. Chernoff had heard of my victory in the Pitzer matter and asked me to handle the Marches trial for him. When I heard the tale of Lou Marches, I knew immediately that Crocker National Bank officials would never allow this story to be heard in a courtroom. It was unbelievable.

Over his lifetime, Louis Marches, seventy-four when the fiasco with Crocker Bank began, had made and lost a little money. He came to Los Angeles in his twenties, looking for stardom. Instead he ended up making a good living in the garment business. He manufactured clothes with beaded pockets. Then beaded pockets went out, and says Louis, "Believe me, there's nobody more gullible than the American public. Beads went out and names came in...." Louis sold his beaded-pocket business and then invested the money in an Arizona produce business. It did not pan out. All that remained was a house he had built at the time the garment business was doing well.

He and his wife had raised three kids and sent them through school. Eventually he sold his house because it was too big for just him and his wife and moved into a rental and bided his time during his retirement.

Meanwhile, he discovered a good deal on a seven-bedroom house in a Los Angeles neighborhood that would probably increase in value as the years went on—mostly because of the city's new interest in preservation. The owners were willing to take $37,500 for it. Louis thought the house was being sold cheap because there were some family problems. He also thought he could spend some money to fix up the place and maybe even turn it into a home for senior citizens. Louis did all the things you have to do to close on the house, including securing a $30,000 mortgage from Crocker.

Every month, when his Social Security check came, he went to his savings bank, cashed it and then went to the nearest Crocker branch, wherever he happened to be, and plunked down his mortgage money. A bank teller would stamp his mortgage book "paid." Everything went well for seven years. Apparently, in September 1980, one payment wasn't recorded.

The computer did not record the cash payment of $195.53 and Crocker claimed Louis was in arrears. Louis made very effort to persuade the bank it was wrong. He talked to anyone at the bank who would listen, showing the date stamped in his coupon book. He pointed out that he had been making his mortgage payments regularly for seven years—sometimes two months at a time. But his pleas fell on deaf ears. Crocker returned the payments Louis made after the disputed month, and claimed it was all or nothing.

Then, during the fifth month, Louis received a different kind of letter. As Louis puts it:

> "Sure enough, they foreclosed. So I took my payment book and the foreclosure papers and I went down to the big main office at Sixth and Olive. I looked on the board for a big shot, like a vice-president or something, and I went up and I saw this

man, the big wheel. I told him my whole story. I told him I didn't want trouble, I wanted peace of mind. Give me peace of mind, I said. I told him my wife was sick and if she found out anything about this it would be terrible, just terrible. Anyway, the big wheel sends me to see another person, a woman. She made copies of my coupon book. She wasn't much help and even said I could sue the bank if I didn't like what was happening. She also told me foreclosure takes three months."

Louis was not too clear about the sequence of events; except that his wife suffered a major stroke the evening of the day someone from the bank called his house and talked to her. Foreclosure and "for sale" signs were tacked up on his property. He remembers that people came around at all hours of the day and night, offering him cash for the house.

Louis was getting angry. He went to see a lawyer who wanted a $3,500 retainer fee before he would file a restraining order.

"So then I said to myself what the hell am I gonna do? I remember. It was a Thursday afternoon, and I decided right then that I'd go that night down to the law library, the county law library and I'd do the whole thing myself. So I went down and the place was full of lawyers, but they wouldn't give me the time of day. So I started looking up restraining orders and I read everything and I copied out this and I copied out that, how to type it, what to say, and I went home and I did it. The next day I went down to the courts and I filed it. It cost me $70. Then I went up to the fifth floor where they told me to go and the clerk there says, 'Just a minute Mr. Marches, I'll go in and see the judge.' Then, twenty minutes later he comes out and he tells me what to do."

The clerk advised Louis to contact the bank's lawyers directly and to tell them to be in court by 2:00 P.M. (There are specified procedures for emergency actions such as these and, since Louis' house was due for foreclosure in just a few days, the judge was acting under those procedures.)

The bank's lawyers took notice of what was going on; they appeared and were ordered to show cause for the foreclosure on Louis's house. Louis showed the lawyers his coupon book, and then everyone went into chambers to discuss the matter with the judge. A clearing date was set for the following Monday.

On Sunday night Louis received a call from one of the bank's lawyers who asked him if they might chat a little outside the courtroom before the hearing. Louis said he didn't think that would be wise—he wanted everything on the record. In the courtroom, according to Louis, the Crocker lawyer was kindness itself. He indicated that Crocker wanted nothing from Louis but the checks the bank had returned to him and for all due payments to be made. They would even absorb the costs, the lawyer explained. So it was all settled and done with, Crocker thought. Louis, however, was not quite finished.

> "I said to the judge, 'Your honor, the reason I didn't want to talk to this man [the lawyer] outside the courtroom is this: I want to know what do I do now?' The judge asks me if I know what recourse I've got and by that I understood him to say I could sue and that's what I did."

Louis went to Stan Chernoff, a lawyer recommended by a friend. They filed a punitive-damage lawsuit against the bank for bad faith by instituting foreclosure proceedings against Louis at a time when its investigations would have revealed the true facts. The suit languished in the courts for a couple of years. Apparently, Crocker Bank looked at it as a nuisance suit. After a year, they offered a small settlement which Chernoff turned down.

A few months before the trial, Chernoff called me. Although his expertise was mostly in real estate and corporate work, a large punitive-damage trial was another matter. After reviewing the case, I realized that it had great emotional appeal. I knew if this case went before a jury, Crocker Bank would be on the wrong end of a very large punitive-damage verdict. There seemed to be no reasonable excuse for what appeared to be most oppressive behavior. This might be a case the bank would want to settle quickly. They would have heard of the Pitzer verdict against Security Pacific and would be too sensitive to allow this story to reach the ears of sympathetic jurors.

I called the bank's attorneys and told them I was now involved in the case and suggested that this was a very serious matter and that they should start looking at it as a dangerous case. They asked for an immediate meeting. The meeting took place in December 1982. I took Louis to the thirty-seventh floor of the Crocker National Bank Building in downtown Los Angeles. We met with two of the bank's lawyers. I made a proposal for an immediate settlement: cancel the mortgage on Louis's house (approximately $18,000) and pay him $250,000 for his trouble.

I recall telling the attorneys that the bank should be ashamed of itself; it ought to be embarrassed because its behavior was so callous. Crocker Bank should not foreclose on an old man and his invalid wife just because they said he had missed a single payment of $195.53. It was their computer screw-up that had caused the problem.

Crocker's attorneys attempted to convince me that a jury would not punish the bank significantly for "making a mistake." I argued that the jury would not consider this a mistake because surely the bank had a duty to investigate all the facts before starting foreclosure proceedings. I reminded them of the specter which a jury would visualize: Crocker Bank's attorneys filing voluminous legal points and authorities against little old Mr. Marches who was making out his own restraining order on his borrowed typewriter with limited knowledge gained at the county law library. I told these attorneys that this would make a classic story and that they had better decide quickly whether they wanted to settle this case or have it to go a jury trial. I gave them ten days to make up their minds.

I took the Christmas holidays off and went to Palm Springs. It wasn't even seven days until the telephone rang. My secretary, Nancy Burnett, told me that the lawyers from Crocker Bank called and decided to give Lou Marches a Christmas present of $250,000, along with canceling his mortgage.

# Chapter 11

# Your Insurance Claim: Some Practical and Legal Tips

## I
## The Insurance Claim Process

Insurance can be boring, and the process of getting your claim paid can be tedious. To make matters worse, you usually must steer through a complicated maze of those eternal claim forms. But, if you want to have some knowledge of the rules of the game and learn some valuable tips, this chapter is for you.

You probably won't learn much from reading your insurance policy because the comprehension level required to understand most insurance policies is slightly above that of Einstein's theory of relativity. No doubt, you start out at a disadvantage. The insurance company deliberately wrote a policy which is difficult to understand, and the company will probably interpret the language to its advantage. Maybe so, but here is an important legal rule that your insurance company won't tell you:

ITEM: COURTS HAVE HELD THAT WHERE INSURANCE POLICY LANGUAGE IS UNCLEAR, THE LANGUAGE WILL BE CONSTRUED AGAINST THE INSURANCE COMPANY.

This rule has been around for over a hundred years and means that where language is capable of two different meanings—yours will prevail. In a dispute, don't take the insurance company's word for the meaning of certain language and phrases in the policy. Stick to your guns if you believe your interpretation of the language is reasonable. Within the last ten years, some courts have gone even farther by holding that:

ITEM: THE REASONABLE EXPECTATIONS OF THE POLICYHOLDER WILL GOVERN THE MEANING OF POLICY LANGUAGE.

This simply means that you get the coverage you expected, so long as your expectation was reasonable. This coverage may exist regardless of some fine print in the policy that may seem contrary.

Most claim denials are based on clauses or phrases called "exclusions." These are the little gems that usually appear on the last several pages of your policy and take away the coverage that appears on the first couple of pages. Because many people are unaware of these exclusions and they are usually difficult to understand, most courts have added another rule to aid the policyholder:

ITEM: EXCLUSIONS IN ANY INSURANCE POLICY MUST BE PHRASED IN PLAIN, CLEAR, AND CONSPICUOUS LANGUAGE. THE BURDEN IS ON THE INSURANCE COMPANY TO PROVE THAT THE EXCLUSION APPLIES AND THAT IT IS CLEAR AND UNDERSTANDABLE.

As you can see, almost all courts have constructed rules to aid the policyholder. This is because most insurance policies are what the law calls adhesion contracts. These are contracts where there is no bargaining. The company offers you a policy on a take-it-or-leave-it basis, and you have no say-so as to what goes into the language of the contract. Don't forget that most insurance adjusters obviously have superior knowledge about insurance, and therefore it is extremely important that you have some understanding of the basic rules of insurance interpretation.

If you are like most people, you won't read your policy carefully until you are ready to file a claim. When you finally sit down to read it, you will discover that buried in a sea of print is a procedure to be followed for filing a claim. You should become familiar with this procedure as a starting point. Most insurance policies spell out requirements for proof of loss as well as time limits in which certain forms have to be filled out and sent in to the company. It would be a good idea to follow these steps religiously. But if you forget to dot the "i" or cross the "t," or if you are late in getting the forms to the company—(even months late)—don't think all is doomed. If the company denies your claim because of some deficiency in filling out the forms or in getting them in on time, write them back and tell them this rule:

ITEM: FAILURE TO PROPERLY FILL OUT INSURANCE FORMS OR GET THEM IN TO THE COMPANY ON TIME IS OF NO CONSEQUENCE TO AN OTHERWISE VALID CLAIM, UNLESS THE INSURANCE COMPANY CAN SHOW IT HAS BEEN HARMED BY THIS FAILURE.

This means that the insurance company has the burden of showing that a deficiency in the claims procedure prevented it from carrying out an adequate investigation or otherwise hurt its ability to handle the claim properly. In most cases, technical deficiencies will not cause an insurance company any problems and should not be used as a reason to deny a claim. Of course, it is always best to file the claim properly and in the company's expected format because then the company is less likely to engage in foot dragging or other delaying tactics, and you will get your claim paid faster.

Many times an insurance claim may be denied without an adequate explanation. Don't settle for this:

ITEM: ALWAYS INSIST ON A WRITTEN EXPLANATION. MOST STATE LAWS REQUIRE AN INSURANCE COMPANY TO PROVIDE YOU WITH A WRITTEN EXPLANATION WHEN A CLAIM IS DENIED. ITS FAILURE TO DO THIS MAY BE AN UNFAIR CLAIMS PRACTICE.

Once you receive the company's written explanation for the denial of your claim, read your policy again. Chances are the company is reading the same words you are, although it may look as though the meanings come from two different dictionaries. With the knowledge you have already gained, you know that language may be interpreted as a lay person would understand it, and policy provisions may be given their most reasonable interpretation according to the expectations of the policyholder. In short, make sure that the reason for the denial of your claim is legitimate. If you have any question or suspicion, dig deeper.

Often your insurance may be part of group insurance. This means that the insurance is purchased through your employment or some group you belong to, like a club or association. The group (employer or association) will receive the master insurance policy, and you, as the employee or club member, may get only a descriptive booklet outlining the coverage. If this happens to you, be sure you save the booklet:

ITEM: IN GROUP POLICIES, THE DESCRIPTIVE BOOKLET OUTLINING THE COVERAGE MAY GOVERN OVER THE FINE PRINT IN THE MASTER POLICY.

Here again, your rights are governed by the words and phrases in the insurance policy. Interpretation and meaning of the language will be critical to you. You should read the explanations provided to you because if there is a dispute over coverage, your interpretation may just carry the day over the insurance company's explanation of what those words mean. Many times, various words are actually defined in the insurance policy. However, more often than not, certain key words or phrases are not. Even where words or phrases are defined, we often discover that the definitions themselves are unclear. Probably the best general guideline to follow is this:

ITEM: TAKE THE INSURANCE COMPANY'S EXPLANATION FOR DENIAL AND TEST IT BY READING YOUR POLICY AND DETERMINING FOR YOURSELF IF THE EXPLANATION IS SATISFACTORY TO YOU. IF IT IS NOT, PURSUE THE MATTER FURTHER.

# II
# When Confronting an Insurance Company, Your Attitude Is Important

Once you file a claim and it has been denied, things become more complicated. You must be prepared mentally for what is going to happen next. If you think that your insurance company has denied your claim wrongfully or has not paid as much on the claim as it should have, speak up. Statistically, insurance companies count on the fact that most people will accept their decisions and will be unwilling or unable to protest. In nine out of ten cases, this is the last the company ever hears from the policyholder. Do not assume that the first no you receive is the final answer. Grandmothers' old adages may keep the wheels turning toward a faster settlement.

ITEM: HONESTY IS THE BEST POLICY.

DON'T PUT OFF UNTIL TOMORROW WHAT YOU CAN DO TODAY.

A SQUEAKY WHEEL GETS THE GREASE.

YOU CAN CATCH MORE FLIES WITH HONEY THAN WITH VINEGAR.

It goes without saying that it is a bad idea to inflate your insurance claim. Padded claims can come back to haunt you one way or another. The most direct impact of an inflated claim may be reflected by the attitude of the claims adjuster. If the claims adjuster thinks the claim is out of line, he may get a chip on his shoulder which will stay there throughout the claim processing. Once the adjuster gets his back up, it will probably make payment of your claim very difficult. Indirectly, inflated claims may boomerang and the company may raise your premium. If you exaggerate a claim intentionally, your insurance company may accuse you of insurance fraud which, in some states, is a very serious criminal charge.

The proper way to start out is to lay all your cards on the table from the beginning. This should be done in a very honest, straightforward, and reasonable fashion. In turn, the company has an obligation to process your claim in good faith. It must treat you and your claim in a reasonable fashion. If it does not, it can be liable for damages and, in some cases, even punitive damages.

# III
# Enlist the Support of
# Your Insurance Agent

If you are having trouble getting your claim paid, contact the agent who sold you the policy. Insurance agents portray themselves as knowledgeable in obtaining coverage for your specific needs. This knowledge creates a legal duty on their part to find and sell the kind of coverage you need.

ITEM: THE AGENT WHO SOLD YOU THE POLICY HAS A DUTY TO OBTAIN THE CORRECT COVERAGE FOR YOU AND TO PROTECT YOUR INTEREST.

Often your agent will go to bat for you by contacting the company's claim department on your behalf. This is particularly true with homeowners and automobile insurance claims since that agent knows you personally and received a commission for selling the policy to you. In order to keep your business and his reputation, he may be willing to act as an intermediary and ombudsman between you and the company. If you have a group policy, there may be an administrator appointed by the company to handle claims from your employer or group. This person usually knows about that particular policy and the claims-processing procedure of that company. Many times a little nudge from these people is all that is needed.

# IV
# How to Communicate with Your Insurance Company

If a phone call or letter to your insurance agent or the company claims representative does not solve the problem, keep going. Be persistent:

> ITEM: IF YOU ARE NOT SATISFIED AT THE LEVEL YOU ARE DEALING WITH, KEEP GOING UP THE LADDER.

At the initial stages, a telephone call may clear up misunderstandings or accidental claims mishandling. There are simple ways to make telephone calls efficiently and to document calls and the substance of the conversation. Have all your papers—your policy, the claim form, the related bills—close at hand when you make the telephone call. Save your telephone bills because a serious insurance problem may require long-distance telephone calls, and the phone bill will prove the call was made and the exact date you spoke to the company.

Always ask for the identity of the person to whom you are speaking and whether he or she has the authority to handle your questions. Keep a telephone log of the dates, times, and telephone numbers. Follow up your conversation with a brief letter to that person, your understanding of the substance of the call, and ask him or her to respond by a certain date if your understanding is incorrect. Even if you are unable to obtain any information of substance, enter into your telephone log what transpired during the conversation.

By the time you have made several phone calls and you feel that you are not making any progress, it is time to state your complaint in writing. Start with the person who denied your claim. Later on, if the matter is still unresolved, you should then write to that person's supervisor or manager. In other words, if you are unable to obtain satisfaction at the level at which you are communicating, try to find out who is at a higher level in the company and communicate with that person. Most companies have claims managers, supervisors, or even consumer complaint departments that will get involved in problem claims and give them special attention. If you have a real gripe and want to reach the top, you may obtain the name and address of the president of each company from the A.M. Best & Co. *Rating Book of Insurance Companies,* which is available in most libraries.

When you write to your insurance company:

(1) Tell them your policy number and explain your concern.

(2) Enclose copies of relevant information like your claim forms and the bills or invoices for which you are claiming coverage.

(3) Insist that the company make a written response to your inquiry and give them a reasonable deadline for reply.

(4) Keep a copy of all correspondence. Never send original material without keeping a copy for yourself.

After the letter is written, allow for a reasonable time for a response. If no response comes within a couple of weeks, write a follow-up letter and enclose a copy of your earlier letter. In most states, insurance companies are obliged to respond to your letters:

ITEM: FAILURE TO ACKNOWLEDGE AND ACT PROMPTLY ON COMMUNICATIONS WITH RESPECT TO CLAIMS IS AN UNFAIR INSURANCE-CLAIMS PRACTICE.

You may be surprised to learn that the insurance company

will often pay your claim after hearing your side of the story. In many cases, the company will offer a compromise which could be a good solution if there is an honest dispute between you and the company. If the company persists in denying your claim, it may give you a further explanation which you may find satisfactory. On the other hand, you may not be able to resolve the dispute to your satisfaction. You will then have two choices. You either forget about it or keep persisting. If you believe that you are right, keep persisting.

# V
# It Is Important to Have
# Good Documentation

It is important to keep good records because they may eventually support a complaint about how your claim was handled. "Be sure you document whom you spoke to and when you talked. And take notes on what was said," advises Robert Hunter, president of the National Insurance Consumer Organization. "It's a little extra work, but it's worth it in the end. It can make all the difference in the world in settling a claim." Here are some tips relating to documenting particular types of coverage disputes. Although this list is not complete, these hints may help with the most frequently encountered claims problems.

*Medical Bills*

Sometimes medical claims are complicated because several parties must participate in processing the claim form. Typically, the policyholder obtains a copy of a claim form from the employer or group policyholder, fills out the individual policyholder's portion, and gives the form to the doctor. The doctor must fill out part of the form and send the form to the insurance carrier or return it to the group policyholder. The problems with having each stage completed properly may range from something as simple as failing to include the date you visited the doctor to something as complicated as explaining why the doctor had to perform additional surgery resulting from complications arising out of the initial procedure. If the insurance company says it needs more medical information, get to the bottom of the problem:

ITEM: DISCUSS THE SITUATION WITH YOUR
DOCTOR'S OFFICE AND GET THE DOCTOR

> INVOLVED. ASK THE DOCTOR'S OFFICE
> TO HELP YOU AND SUPPLY THE
> COMPANY WITH THIS DOCUMENTATION
> YOURSELF.

Many times you will discover that further clarification from the doctor's office will do the trick. If not, it is always good to have supporting communication from the doctor's office in your file.

### Personal Property and Auto Claims

With personal property claims, the value of the loss is sometimes difficult to prove by documentation. Although your homeowner's policy will cover some personal property losses, you should insure valuables such as antiques, jewelry, furs and works of art separately under special riders to your policy. In any event:

> ITEM: MAKE SURE YOU HAVE AN UP-TO-DATE
> INVENTORY OF EVERYTHING YOU
> INSURE.

It is a good idea to take pictures of each room to show each item. Whenever possible, keep sales receipts showing the date and price of each item. Stash these receipts in a secure place away from the house, such as a safe-deposit box, where they will be safe in case of a fire or burglary. Even if you have not kept a receipt, you may be able to document the purchase price by a copy of your canceled check or your credit-card charge receipt.

Consumer-education efforts have now impressed drivers with the importance of obtaining pictures and estimates of damage to automobiles. As with any documentation, however, do not send original copies of a photograph without keeping one for yourself. The same thing holds for estimates, service-station receipts, towing-service charges, and repair bills. Disputes over the value of a car involved in a theft or accident are fairly common. Service receipts, a repair history including a record of all the work done on your car including regular maintenance service and mileage is invaluable when you are trying to establish the condition of your car after your car has been lost or destroyed. In addition to the particular condition of your own car, there are general guidelines for the value of each make and model.

Make sure you are getting fair value for your car if the company wants to write if off or "total" it. One way to do this is to check the amount against the value listed in *The Kelly Blue Book*. This book is used widely throughout the auto industry to establish the value of used cars. It is published by Kelly Blue Book Company, 2950 A7 Airway Avenue, Costa Mesa, California 92626; anyone can purchase one. This book provides powerful information concerning the value of your car because these are the values that are generally accepted in the auto industry, and it may be unfair for an insurance company to offer you less.

### Disability Insurance Claims

Disability insurance claims are often confusing because state laws may define disability in one way while the insurance company defines it in another way. Insurance companies sell policies nationwide with uniform descriptions of disability even though this definition is not always valid under the various states' law. For example, in California people are considered totally disabled if they are unable to work with reasonable continuity in their customary occupation or in any other occupation in which they might reasonably be expected to engage, considering their past employment, education, and physical and mental capacity, including the opportunities on the job market. Even so, many insurance companies sell disability coverage in California using a definition of disability which says that people are disabled only if they are unable to engage in any occupation or employment at any level:

> ITEM: BE SURE THAT YOUR DOCTOR UNDER-
> STANDS YOUR JOB DESCRIPTION,
> YOUR EMPLOYMENT HISTORY, AND YOUR
> EDUCATION IN ORDER TO EVALUATE
> WHETHER, CONSIDERING YOUR PHY-
> SICAL CONDITION, YOU REASONABLY
> MAY BE EXPECTED TO WORK.

In short, you must document the nature of your injury and how it affects your ability to work, both with your doctor and your employer. If your employer will not take you back to work, or will take you back only on a trial basis, make sure that your insurance company understands the situation with good documentation.

# VI
# What To Do If Your Claim Is Documented Properly and You Are Still Unsatisfied

1. *You may want to contact your State Department of Insurance.*

If your effort at negotiating with a company has been unsuccessful, you may want to contact your state insurance department. Some states such as New York and Illinois have strong, well-staffed insurance departments that take an active interest in consumer disputes. California conducts investigations on individual complaints. However, many states lack the resources and interest to become involved in individual complaints or are too overwhelmed by the insurance lobby to set up an active consumer advocacy.

In any event, most state departments of insurance will listen to your complaint and contact the insurance company to see whether they can resolve the problem. Although a state department of insurance will not be able to get you damages, as in a court of law, many times it is successful in getting your claim paid or at least settled. However, if this tactic does not work, it is not the end of the line. It is now time for stronger measures.

2. *You may want to consider Small Claims Court.*

If your claim is less than the jurisdictional amount of the small claims court in your state, you can take the company directly to court yourself without the assistance of a lawyer and frequently obtain quick results. The jurisdictional amount of small claims court is usually low, often in the neighborhood of $1,000. Remember, when you are listing your damages for the failure to pay the claim, that you may be entitled to mileage costs, incidental damages for postage, paperwork processing, telephone calls, and the loss of the use of the money for the time period the company withheld it wrongfully. If you are willing to go to small claims court and your claim is for slightly more than the maximum limit of the court, to save time and expense, you may wish, to reduce your claim to the jurisdictional limit; for example, if the small claims jurisdiction limit is $1,500 and your medical bills are $1,600, you may file your small claims for $1,500 and forgive the extra $100. A small-claims lawsuit will require the company to find someone to go to court for it, and this costs the company time and money. The very fact you are willing to go to court may force the company to settle with you.

3. *If all else fails, see a lawyer.*

Finding and retaining a lawyer may not be as hard or costly as you think. Local bar associations and consumer-advocate groups may be able to refer you to a lawyer who is familiar with insurance company practices. Although much legal work is done by lawyers who charge a certain fee per hour, in most cases insurance claims can be handled by lawyers who will work on a contingency basis. If you don't want to lay out money for a lawyer, the contingency fee is for you.

> ITEM: A CONTINGENCY FEE PERMITS THE POLICYHOLDER TO OBTAIN REPRESENTATION AND PAY THE LAWYER A PERCENTAGE OF WHAT THE LAWYER EVENTUALLY RECOVERS. IF THE POLICYHOLDER DOES NOT RECOVER ANY DAMAGES, THE POLICYHOLDER DOES NOT PAY THE LAWYER.

There are many lawyers who are willing to take this type of case on a contingency basis. Generally, these lawyers are called trial lawyers. You can obtain information about trial lawyers in your state by writing to the Association of Trial Lawyers of America, 1050 31st Street, N.W., Washington, D.C. 20007.

This organization has a directory of its members who take cases mostly on a contingency-fee basis and who generally represent people who have problems with insurance companies. In addition, most states have state trial-lawyer organizations. These organizations will be happy to provide information about members. For example, the California Trial Lawyers Association is headquartered at 1020 12th Street, Sacramento, California 95814 and will send you information about trial lawyers in local California communities.

An important item when shopping for a lawyer is cost and quality, just like shopping for anything else. Do a little homework about your lawyer—check out his competence in this area—and make sure you understand the fee agreement before you sign a retainer. When you go to the lawyer's office for your initial interview, be sure you take any booklet or advertising material that relates to the insurance policy, the policy itself if you have it, a copy of the claims form you submitted, and all supporting documentation, and the records of all your correspondence with the company. Be prepared to discuss all aspects of your claim in order to enable the lawyer to evaluate your case.

When an insurance company has denied a claim wrongfully, the policyholder and his family may experience emotional distress and other damages such as economic loss. In order to evaluate whether your case has merit, your lawyer will need adequate, truthful information on all aspects of your complaint. Be sure to tell the lawyer all of the hardships you have suffered because your claim was denied. Remember that lawyers have not been trained in psychiatry or medicine, and the reaches of the lawyers' skills may not extend to all the personal problems and financial strain caused by the claim's denial.

# VII
# What Happens If the Company Handled a Claim in Bad Faith?

To put it simply, "bad faith" is the unreasonable refusal to promptly pay a valid claim. Bad faith can also encompass a company's failure to investigate a claim adequately or its unreasonable delay in claims processing or its inadequate payment for the claim filed. Ordinarily, a policyholder is entitled only to the benefits set out in the policy, but:

ITEM: IF THE INSURANCE COMPANY BREACHED THE DUTY OF GOOD FAITH IT OWES YOU, YOU, AS A POLICYHOLDER, MAY ALSO BE ENTITLED TO RECOVER INCIDENTAL DAMAGES INCLUDING ECONOMIC LOSS AND A SUM FOR EMOTIONAL DISTRESS. IF THE COMPANY HAS BEEN REALLY ROTTEN, THE LAW MAY PROVIDE FOR PUNITIVE DAMAGES.

The law established punitive damages to serve as a deterrent to bad-claims practices. Not all states have punitive-damages laws, but most states have some type of laws to protect policyholders from unfair claims practices and also allow other types of penalties or damages to be imposed.

A new case came down from the United States Supreme Court in 1987 which may have taken the right away from policyholders to sue for bad faith dealings in situations where their insurance coverage was provided under group plans through employers. Although there may be some exceptions to this rule, it looks very probable in the future that policyholders who happen to have group coverage through their employers, rather than individual policies, could be the victims of bad faith, fraud or other dishonest dealings and not be able to seek any damages for such illegal activities. That case, entitled *Dudeaux vs. Pilot Life*, seems to hold that the only remedy for the policyholder will be to seek actual damages under a federal law which does not provide for consequential or punitive damages. It appears likely and logical that the Congress will soon be implored to amend that federal law.

The cases in this book were the cases of individuals who took their complaints all the way through jury trials. If you take your case all the way, the chances are that a jury of your peers will decide correctly which side is right. If you are, it will decide on the amount you should receive. Don't be afraid to let a jury resolve your dispute. It is the fairest and most democratic institution in our society.

# VIII
# Don't Sleep on Your Rights

Sleeping on your rights is bad for you, your family, and society. The purpose of this book is to make you aware of certain valuable rights and to show you how average citizens have used these rights effectively. Whether you use this knowledge is up to you. As Barbara Visconti said from her deathbed (Chapter 3), "We are victims because we allow ourselves to become victims."

Exercising your rights is extremely significant to you and your family because without the knowledge and ability to fight back, sooner or later, you increase the risk of becoming a victim of insurance abuse. Doing nothing only guarantees that you will come out a sure loser. On the other hand, being able to handle yourself effectively will probably get you what is rightly due you and, in some cases of insurance abuse, even more as a form of punishment to the offending company.

More importantly, we are in an era of heavy emphasis on a free marketplace unregulated by government controls. This is true particularly of the insurance industry, although it applies to many other industries as well. The only way for a free marketplace to stay healthy indefinitely is to have a mechanism for catching and punishing those who abuse the privileges of a free marketplace. This means that you, the consumer—when you become a victim—have a duty, for the sake of society, to exercise your rights and, in so doing, keep our free marketplace honest and healthy.

By the same token, you must guard against abuse by us —the consumer. Just as a cake can be overdone, so can consumer and lawyers do more harm than good to a healthy system by making outrageous claims or bringing frivolous lawsuits. It is precisely this type of thing, particularly the extreme cases, that are used as examples by the insurance industry to make its case for reform of the system. What the insurance industry means by reform is usually a taking away or watering down of our valuable rights. Just look at the advertisements the insurance companies are placing in our national magazines. They want to do away with everything from punitive damages to the jury trial itself. What they don't realize is that they may be sowing the seeds of their own destruction because when there are no meaningful rights left for the consumer to exercise, sooner or later unscrupulous commercial conduct will get so blatant that governmental regulators will be back in full force.

Although it has become quite popular to denounce our litigious society and to condemn lawyers and claimants seeking relief in courts as overzealous and even greedy, the civil suit seeking punitive damages for wrongful conduct is the most effective weapon available to citizens against abuse by insurance companies and other corporations. Rarely has the need to haul these corporate malefactors into account been more urgent.

Most of the cases in this book and thousands of other punitive-damages cases around the country expose the willingness of numerous insurance companies to place greed over public responsibility.

The consumer who is well informed and who is willing to exercise his rights when the occasion demands will make our system work and keep it healthy. This book is dedicated to that consumer.

# APPENDIX

This list contains the offices of various trial lawyer associations found in all states. Many of these associations have referral services that will provide the names and telephone numbers of individual lawyers who are experienced in handling insurance claims on behalf of policyholders.

ALABAMA TRIAL LAWYERS
ASSOCIATION
750 Washington Avenue
Suite 210
Montgomery, AL 36104
205-262-4974

ALASKA TRIAL LAWYERS
ASSOCIATION
805 West 3rd Avenue
Suite A
Anchorage, AK 99501
907-258-4040

ARIZONA TRIAL LAWYERS
ASSOCIATION
1001 North Central Avenue
Suite 590
Phoenix, AZ 85004
602-257-8236

ARKANSAS TRIAL LAWYERS
ASSOCIATION
1700 First Commercial
Building
Little Rock, AR 72201
501-372-5847

CALIFORNIA TRIAL LAWYERS
ASSOCIATION
1020 Twelfth Street
4th Floor
Sacramento, CA 95814
916-442-6902

LOS ANGELES TRIAL LAWYERS
ASSOCIATION
2140 West Olympic Boulevard
Suite 324
Los Angeles, CA 90006
213-487-1212

ORANGE COUNTY TRIAL LAWYERS
ASSOCIATION
888 North Main Street
Suite 905
Santa Ana, CA 92701
714-836-7791

SAN DIEGO TRIAL LAWYERS
ASSOCIATION
2247 San Diego Avenue
Suite 136
San Diego, CA 92110
619-299-7757

SAN FRANCISCO TRIAL LAWYERS
ASSOCIATION
World Trade Center
Ferry Building
Suite 230
San Francisco, CA 94111
415-956-6401

COLORADO TRIAL LAWYERS
ASSOCIATION
1888 Sherman Street
Suite 370
Denver, CO 80203
303-831-1192

CONNECTICUT TRIAL LAWYERS
ASSOCIATION
563 Broad Street
Hartford, CT 06106
203-522-4345

DELAWARE TRIAL LAWYERS
ASSOCIATION
P.O. Box 1145
Wilmington, DE 19899
302-652-6635

TRIAL LAWYERS ASSOCIATION OF
THE DISTRICT OF COLUMBIA
1818 N Street, N.W.
Suite 250
Washington, DC 20036
202-659-3532

THE ACADEMY OF FLORIDA
TRIAL LAWYERS
218 South Monroe Street
Tallahassee, FL 32301
904-224-9403

GEORGIA TRIAL LAWYERS
ASSOCIATION
41 Marietta Street
Suite 714
Atlanta, GA 30303
404-522-8487

IDAHO TRIAL LAWYERS
ASSOCIATION
P.O. Box 1777
Boise, ID 83701
208-345-1890

ILLINOIS TRIAL LAWYERS
ASSOCIATION
110 West Edwards Street
P.O. Box 5000
Springfield, IL 62705
217-789-0755

INDIANA TRIAL LAWYERS
309 West Washington Street
Suite 207
Indianapolis, IN 46204
317-634-8841

ASSOCIATION OF TRIAL
LAWYERS OF IOWA
526 Fleming Building
Des Moines, IA 50309
515-280-7366

KANSAS TRIAL LAWYERS
ASSOCIATION
112 West Sixth
Suite 311
Topeka, KS 66603
913-232-7756

KENTUCKY ACADEMY OF
TRIAL LAWYERS
200 Cumberland Building
12700 Shelbyville Road
Louisville, KY 40243
502-244-1320

LOUISIANA TRIAL LAWYERS
ASSOCIATION
442 Europe Street
P.O. Drawer 4289
Baton Rouge, LA 70821
504-383-5554

MAINE TRIAL LAWYERS
ASSOCIATION
34 Parkwood Drive
P.O. Box 428
Augusta, ME 04330
207-623-2661

MARYLAND TRIAL LAWYERS
ASSOCIATION
201 East Preston
Baltimore, MD 21202
301-539-4336

MASSACHUSETTS ACADEMY OF
TRIAL LAWYERS
59 Temple Place
Suite 410
Boston, MA 02111
617-350-0146

MICHIGAN TRIAL LAWYERS
ASSOCIATION
501 South Capitol Avenue
Suite 405
Lansing, MI 48933
517-482-7740

MINNESOTA TRIAL LAWYERS
ASSOCIATION
906 Midwest Plaza East
Minneapolis, MN 55402
612-375-1707

MISSISSIPPI TRIAL LAWYERS
ASSOCIATION
727 North Congress Street
P.O. Box 1992
Jackson, MS 39205
601-948-8631

MISSOURI ASSOCIATION OF
TRIAL LAWYERS
312 Monroe Street
2nd Floor
P.O. Box 1792
Jefferson City, MO 65102
314-635-5215

MONTANA TRIAL LAWYERS
ASSOCIATION
#1 Last Chance Gulch
Helena, MT 59601
406-443-3124

NEBRASKA ASSOCIATION OF
TRIAL LAWYERS
605 South 14th Street
Suite 450A
Lincoln, NE 68508
402-435-5526

NEVADA TRIAL LAWYERS
ASSOCIATION
205 South Minnesota Street
Carson City, NV 89703
702-883-3577

NEW HAMPSHIRE TRIAL
LAWYERS ASSOCIATION
2½ Beacon Street
P.O. Box 447
Concord, NH 03302
603-224-7077

ATLA NEW JERSEY
15 South Main Street
Edison, NJ 08837
201-906-8444

NEW MEXICO TRIAL LAWYERS
ASSOCIATION
P.O. Box 301
Albuquerque, NM 87103
505-243-6003

NEW YORK STATE TRIAL
LAWYERS ASSOCIATION, INC.
132 Nassau Street
New York, NY 10038
212-349-5890

NORTH CAROLINA ACADEMY
OF TRIAL LAWYERS
208 Fayetteville Mall
P.O. Box 767
Raleigh, NC 27602
919-832-1413

NORTH DAKOTA TRIAL
LAWYERS ASSOCIATION
P.O. Box 2359
Bismarck, ND 58502
701-258-9530

OHIO ACADEMY OF
TRIAL LAWYERS
1024 Dublin Road
Columbus, OH 43215
614-488-3151

OKLAHOMA TRIAL
LAWYERS ASSOCIATION
323 NE 27th
Oklahoma City, OK 73105
405-525-8044

OREGON TRIAL LAWYERS
ASSOCIATION
1020 SW Taylor Street
Suite 750
Portland, OR 97205
503-223-5587

PENNSYLVANIA TRIAL
LAWYERS ASSOCIATION
230 South Broad Street
18th Floor
Philadelphia, PA 19102
215-546-6451

PHILADELPHIA TRIAL LAWYERS
ASSOCIATION
230 South Broad Street
18th Floor
Philadelphia, PA 19102
215-732-2256

RHODE ISLAND TRIAL
LAWYERS ASSOCIATION
Twelve Barnes Street
Smithfield, RI 02828
401-272-8855

SOUTH CAROLINA TRIAL
LAWYERS ASSOCIATION
P.O. Box 11557
Columbia, SC 29211
803-799-5097

SOUTH DAKOTA TRIAL
LAWYERS ASSOCIATION
207 East Capitol
Suite 206
P.O. Box 1154
Pierre, SD 57501
605-224-9292

TENNESSEE TRIAL
LAWYERS ASSOCIATION
629 Woodland Street
Nashville, TN 37206
615-254-1986

TEXAS TRIAL LAWYERS
ASSOCIATION
1220 Colorado
Austin, TX 78701
512-476-3852

UTAH TRIAL LAWYERS
ASSOCIATION
141 West Haven Avenue
Suite 2
Salt Lake City, UT 84115
801-487-4841

VERMONT TRIAL LAWYERS
ASSOCIATION
P.O. Box 5359
Burlington, VT 05402
802-865-4700

VIRGINIA TRIAL LAWYERS
ASSOCIATION
700 East Main Street
Suite 1510
Richmond, VA 23219
804-343-1143

WASHINGTON STATE TRIAL
LAWYERS ASSOCIATION
225 South Washington
Seattle, WA 98104
206-464-1011

WEST VIRGINIA TRIAL LAWYERS
ASSOCIATION
P.O. Box 3968
Charleston, WV 25339
304-344-0692

WISCONSIN ACADEMY OF
TRIAL LAWYERS
44 East Mifflin Street
Madison, WI 53703
608-257-5741

WYOMING TRIAL LAWYERS
ASSOCIATION
2601 Central Avenue
Suite 100
Cheyenne, WY 82001
307-635-0820

TRIAL LAWYERS ASSOCIATION
OF BRITISH COLUMBIA
464-1155 West Georgia Street
Vancouver, British Columbia
Canada V6E 3H4
604-682-5343

SASKATCHEWAN TRIAL
LAWYERS ASSOCIATION
137 Meighen Crescent
Saskatoon, Saskatchewan
Canada S7L 4W3
306-382-8663

In California, the INSURANCE CONSUMER ACTION NETWORK (ICAN) is an organization that helps policyholders. For further information, contact Steven L. Miller, Executive Director, INSURANCE CONSUMER ACTION NETWORK, 3580 Wilshire Boulevard, 17th Floor, Los Angeles, California 90010; 213-387-2515.

Mr. Shernoff's law firm in Claremont, California, has a staff of insurance analysts that will assist policyholders and answer questions concerning insurance coverage and disputes. Correspondence can be directed to Insurance Analysts, Shernoff, Scott & Bidart, 600 South Indian Hill Boulevard, Claremont, California 91711; or policyholders can call 714-621-4935.

# INDEX